art spiegelman

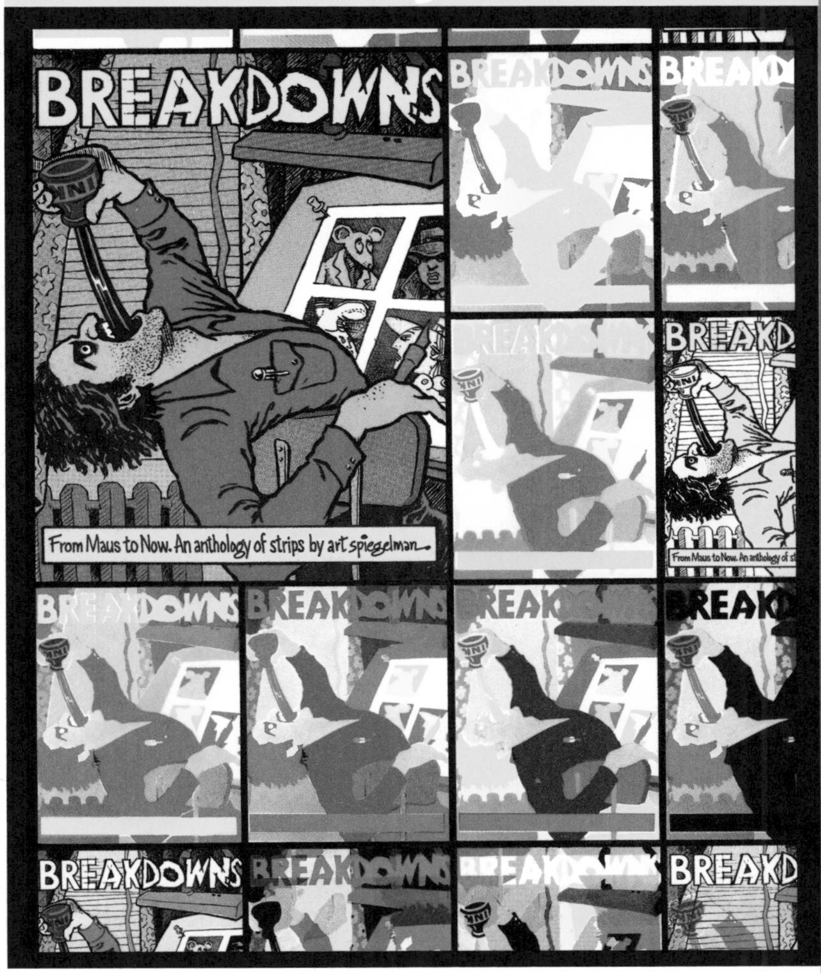
BREAKDOWNS
From Maus to Now. An anthology of strips by art spiegelman

BREAKDOWNS

PORTRAIT OF THE ARTIST AS A YOUNG %@?★!

FOR FRANÇOISE

(AND IN MEMORY OF WOODY GELMAN)

ALL RIGHTS RESERVED. PUBLISHED IN THE UNITED STATES BY PANTHEON BOOKS, A DIVISION OF RANDOM HOUSE, INC., NEW YORK,
AND IN CANADA BY RANDOM HOUSE OF CANADA LIMITED, TORONTO.
PANTHEON BOOKS AND COLOPHON ARE REGISTERED TRADEMARKS OF RANDOM HOUSE, INC.
A PREVIOUS EDITION OF THIS WORK WAS PUBLISHED IN DIFFERENT FORM BY BELIER PRESS, NEW YORK, IN 1977.
A CATALOGUING-IN-PUBLICATION RECORD FOR THIS WORK HAS BEEN ESTABLISHED BY THE LIBRARY OF CONGRESS.

ISBN 978-0-375-42395-6
WWW.PANTHEONBOOKS.COM
PRINTED IN SINGAPORE
FIRST REVISED EDITION

246897531

BREAKDOWNS

PORTRAIT OF THE ARTIST AS A YOUNG %@&*!

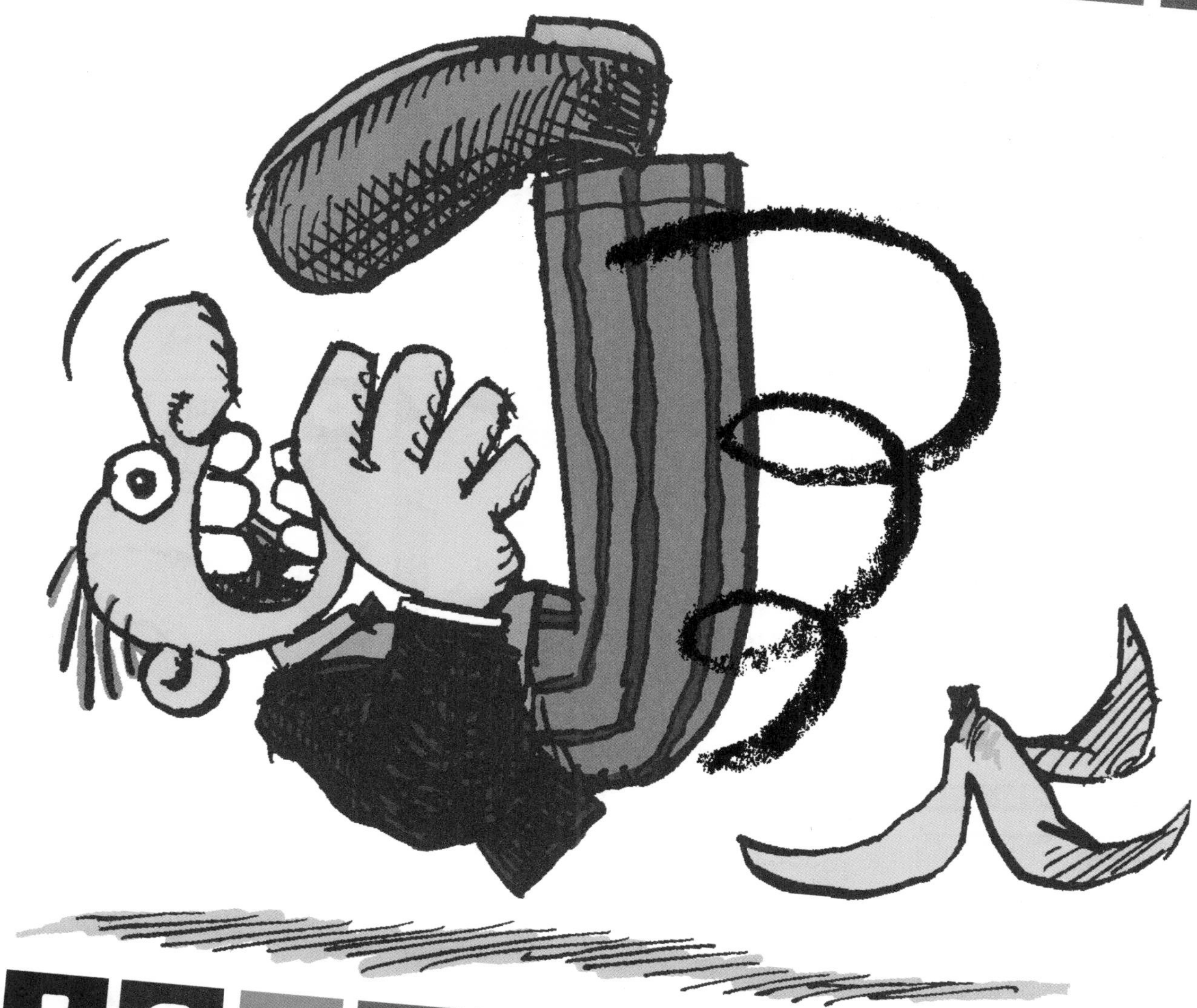

SPIEGELMAN

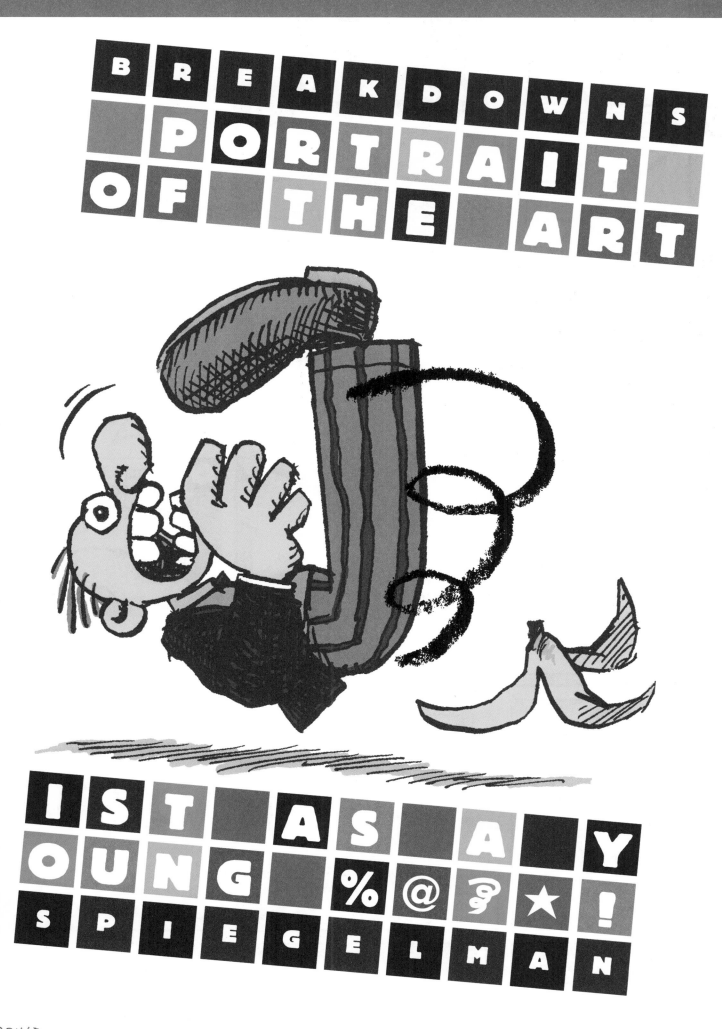

PANTHEON BOOKS

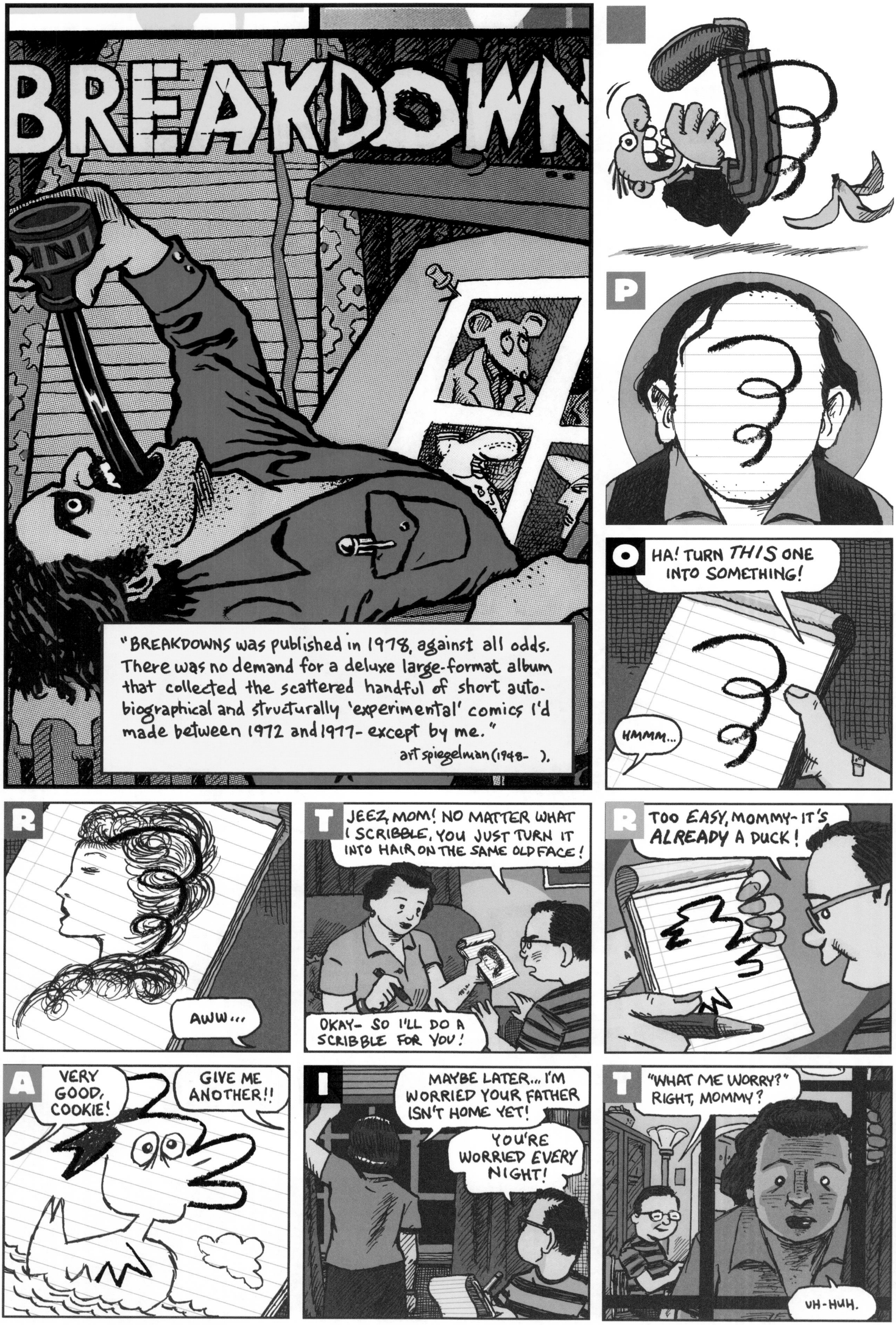
BREAKDOWN
"BREAKDOWNS was published in 1978, against all odds. There was no demand for a deluxe large-format album that collected the scattered handful of short auto-biographical and structurally 'experimental' comics I'd made between 1972 and 1977- except by me."
art spiegelman (1948-).
P
O
HA! TURN THIS ONE INTO SOMETHING!
HMMM...
R
AWW...
T
JEEZ, MOM! NO MATTER WHAT I SCRIBBLE, YOU JUST TURN IT INTO HAIR ON THE SAME OLD FACE!
OKAY- SO I'LL DO A SCRIBBLE FOR YOU!
R
TOO EASY, MOMMY- IT'S ALREADY A DUCK!
A
VERY GOOD, COOKIE!
GIVE ME ANOTHER!!
I
MAYBE LATER... I'M WORRIED YOUR FATHER ISN'T HOME YET!
YOU'RE WORRIED EVERY NIGHT!
T
"WHAT ME WORRY?" RIGHT, MOMMY?
UH-HUH.

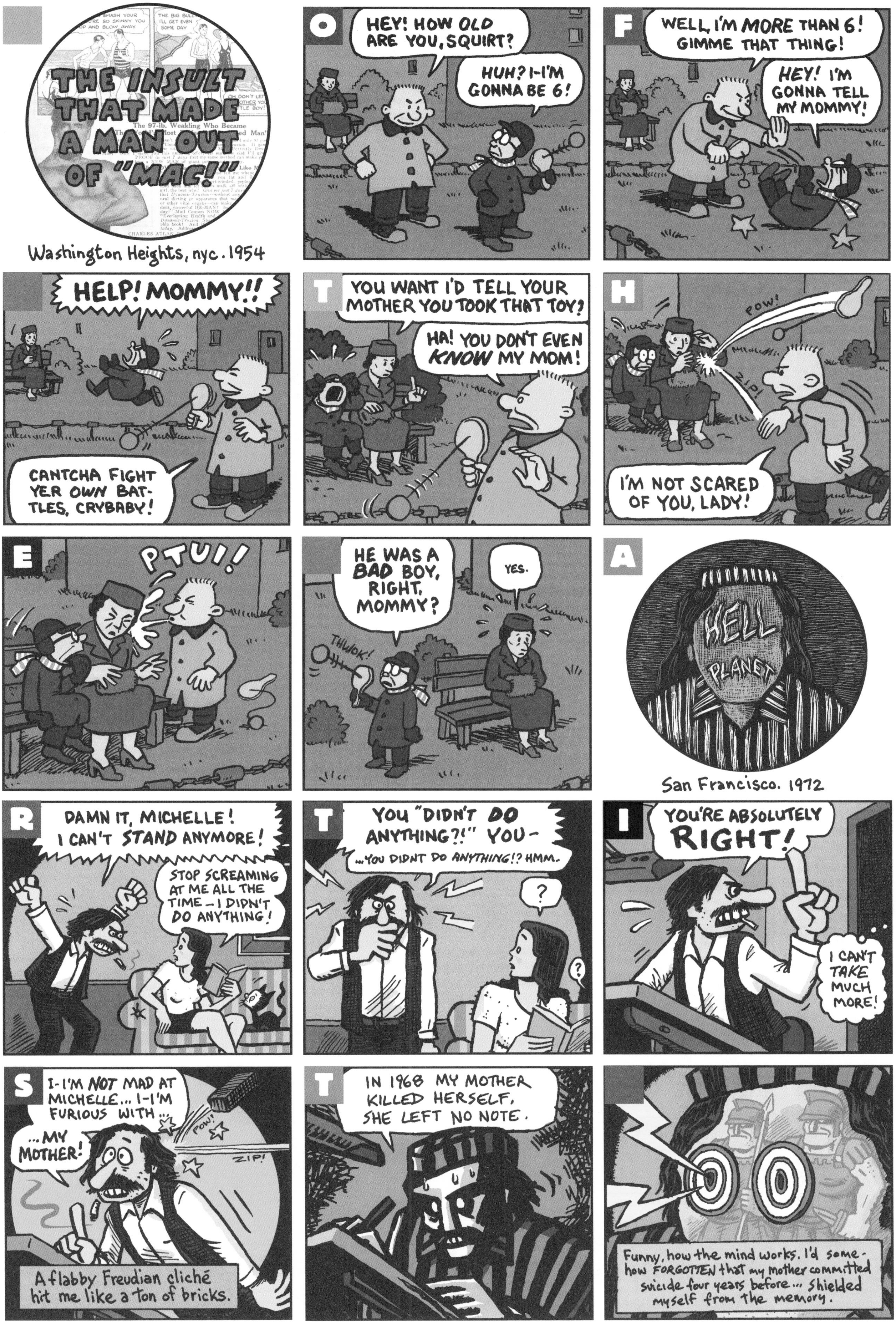

THE INSULT THAT MADE A MAN OUT OF "MAC!"
Washington Heights, nyc. 1954
O
HEY! HOW OLD ARE YOU, SQUIRT?
HUH? I-I'M GONNA BE 6!
F
WELL, I'M MORE THAN 6! GIMME THAT THING!
HEY! I'M GONNA TELL MY MOMMY!
HELP! MOMMY!!
CANTCHA FIGHT YER OWN BAT-TLES, CRYBABY!
T
YOU WANT I'D TELL YOUR MOTHER YOU TOOK THAT TOY?
HA! YOU DON'T EVEN KNOW MY MOM!
H
POW!
ZIP!
I'M NOT SCARED OF YOU, LADY!
E
PTUI!
HE WAS A BAD BOY, RIGHT, MOMMY?
YES.
THWOK!
A
HELL PLANET
San Francisco. 1972
R
DAMN IT, MICHELLE! I CAN'T STAND ANYMORE!
STOP SCREAMING AT ME ALL THE TIME — I DIDN'T DO ANYTHING!
T
YOU "DIDN'T DO ANYTHING?!" YOU—
...YOU DIDNT DO ANYTHING!? HMM.
?
?
I
YOU'RE ABSOLUTELY RIGHT!
I CAN'T TAKE MUCH MORE!
S
I-I'M NOT MAD AT MICHELLE... I-I'M FURIOUS WITH...
...MY MOTHER!
POW!
ZIP!
A flabby Freudian cliché hit me like a ton of bricks.
T
IN 1968 MY MOTHER KILLED HERSELF. SHE LEFT NO NOTE.
Funny, how the mind works. I'd somehow FORGOTTEN that my mother committed suicide four years before... Shielded myself from the memory.

Other work came to a halt while I feverishly brought "Hell Planet" into focus. At first I thought it might be too personal—too fraught—to publish...but comics just aren't complete 'til they're printed...

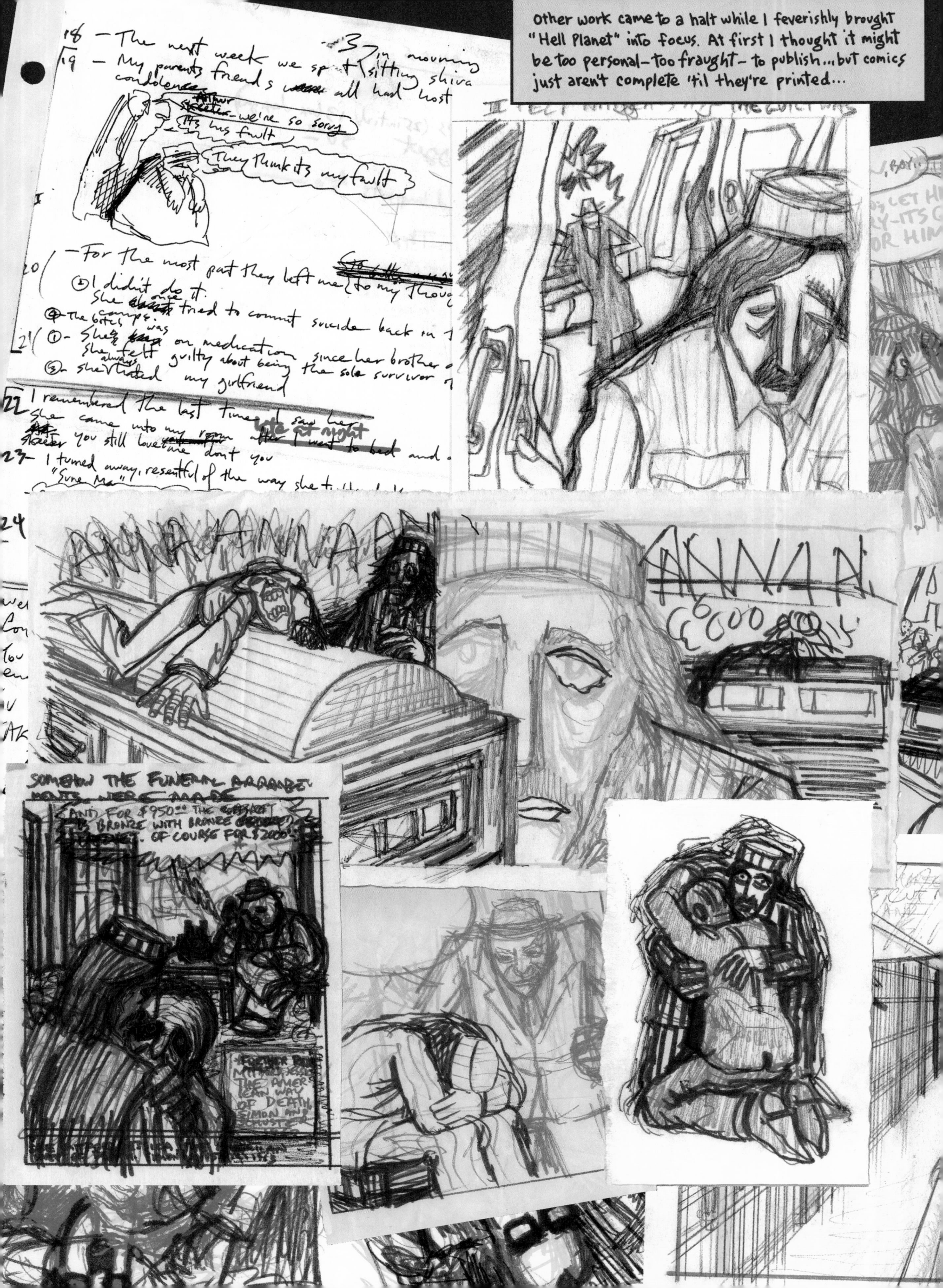

18 — The next week we spent
19 — My parents friends all had lost
Arthur — we're so sorry
It's his fault
They think it's my fault
20 — For the most part they left me to my thoug
① I didn't do it.
She once tried to commit suicide back in t
21 ① — She was on medication since her brother
She felt guilty about being the sole survivor o
③ — She always hated my girlfriend
22 I remembered the last time I saw her
She came into my room after I went to bed and
Skeeter you still love me don't you
23 — I turned away, resentful of the way she
"Sure Ma"
ANNA ANNA
ANNA
SOMEHOW THE FUNERAL ARRANGEMENTS WERE MADE
THE AMERICAN WAY OF DEATH
SIMON AND SCHUSTER

"Just a Piece o' Shit" (a four-page story about a talking turd), an aptly named specimen of the artist's early work. Inset: His cover for the underground comic where it and "Prisoner on the Hell Planet" were both first published.

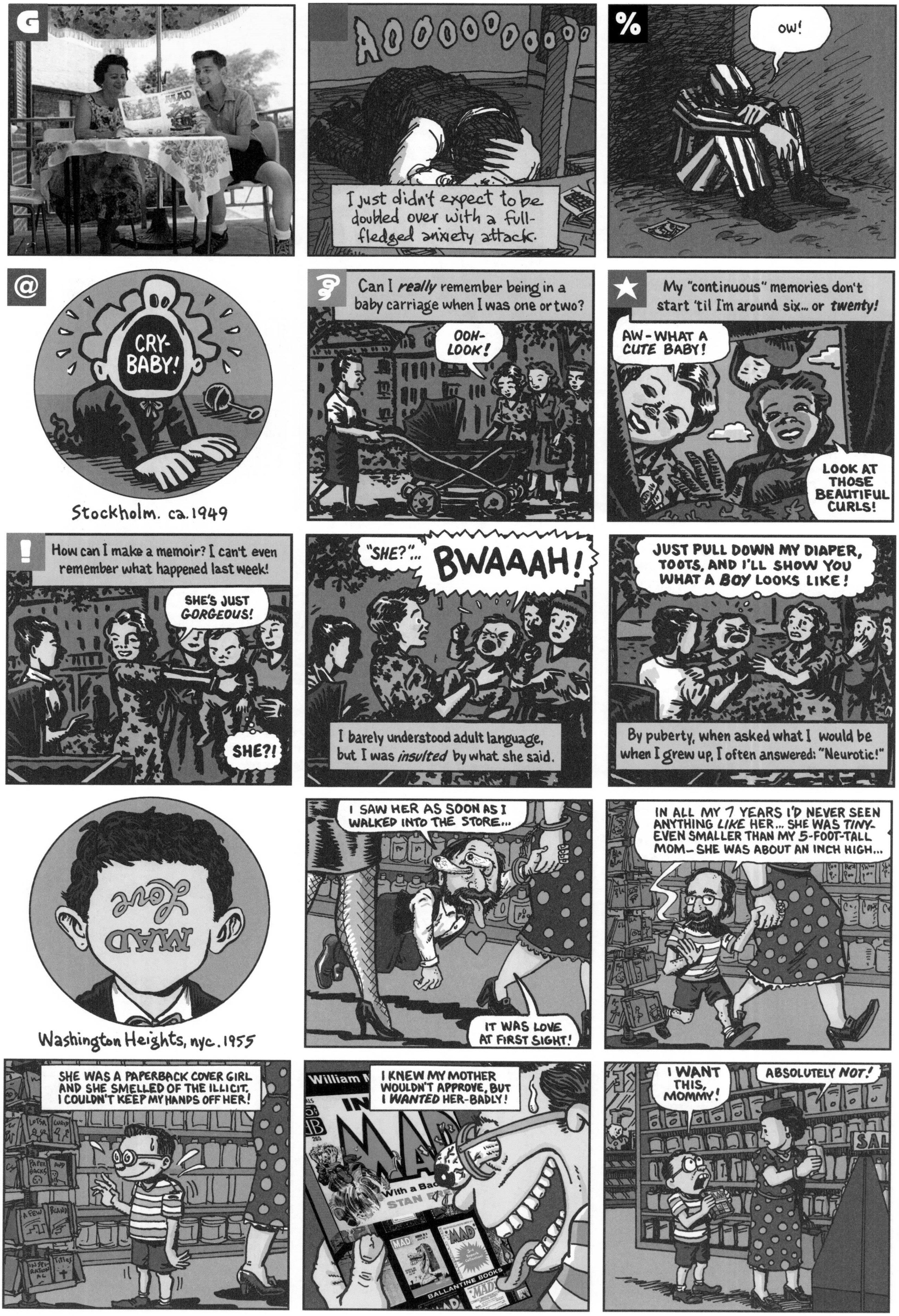
AOOOOOoooo
I just didn't expect to be doubled over with a full-fledged anxiety attack.
OW!
CRY-BABY!
Stockholm. ca.1949
Can I *really* remember being in a baby carriage when I was one or two?
OOH-LOOK!
My "continuous" memories don't start 'til I'm around six... or *twenty!*
AW-WHAT A CUTE BABY!
LOOK AT THOSE BEAUTIFUL CURLS!
How can I make a memoir? I can't even remember what happened last week!
SHE'S JUST *GORGEOUS!*
SHE?!
"SHE?"...
BWAAAH!
I barely understood adult language, but I was *insulted* by what she said.
JUST PULL DOWN MY DIAPER, TOOTS, AND I'LL SHOW YOU WHAT A *BOY* LOOKS LIKE!
By puberty, when asked what I would be when I grew up, I often answered: "Neurotic!"
Washington Heights, nyc. 1955
I SAW HER AS SOON AS I WALKED INTO THE STORE...
IT WAS LOVE AT FIRST SIGHT!
IN ALL MY 7 YEARS I'D NEVER SEEN ANYTHING *LIKE* HER... SHE WAS *TINY*- EVEN SMALLER THAN MY 5-FOOT-TALL MOM- SHE WAS ABOUT AN INCH HIGH...
SHE WAS A PAPERBACK COVER GIRL AND SHE SMELLED OF THE ILLICIT, I COULDN'T KEEP MY HANDS OFF HER!
I KNEW MY MOTHER WOULDN'T APPROVE, BUT I *WANTED* HER-BADLY!
MAD
BALLANTINE BOOKS
I WANT THIS, MOMMY!
ABSOLUTELY *NOT!*

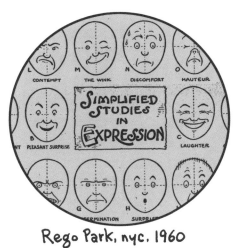

DESPITE MY MODEST DRAWING SKILLS I *HAD* TO BECOME A CARTOONIST... ANYTHING ELSE WOULD HAVE SET ME BACK A MONTH'S ALLOWANCE!

RUEFUL   DEAD

Genius

Rego Park, nyc.

I don't remember *when* she said it, but it still echoes inside...

YOU KNOW, ARTIE...

MAYBE IT'S *BETTER* TO NOT BE A GENIUS...

AFTER ALL, GENIUSES LEAD SUCH TROUBLED LIVES!

OW!

Discovering America

SUPER DUCK

Rego Park, nyc. ca. 1958

Everything I know I learned from comic books...

WOW! LOOKIT THIS AD!

IT'S BIG ENOUGH FOR 2-3 KIDS *AND* IT'S WATERPROOF!

$1.00 SEEMS TOO **CHEAP** FOR SUCH A HOUSE, SWEETIE.

CHEAP? IT COSTS AS MUCH AS *TEN* COMIC BOOKS-BUT I'M GONNA SAVE UP! IT'S A BARGAIN 'CUZ YOU BUY DIRECTLY FROM THE FACTORY!

I'LL PUT IT IN THE YARD AND *SLEEP* IN IT. MAYBE DAD'LL EVEN LET ME GET A **DOG** AND USE IT AS A *DOGHOUSE!*

EVEN *BEFORE* AUSCHWITZ YOUR FATHER WAS AFRAID OF DOGS.

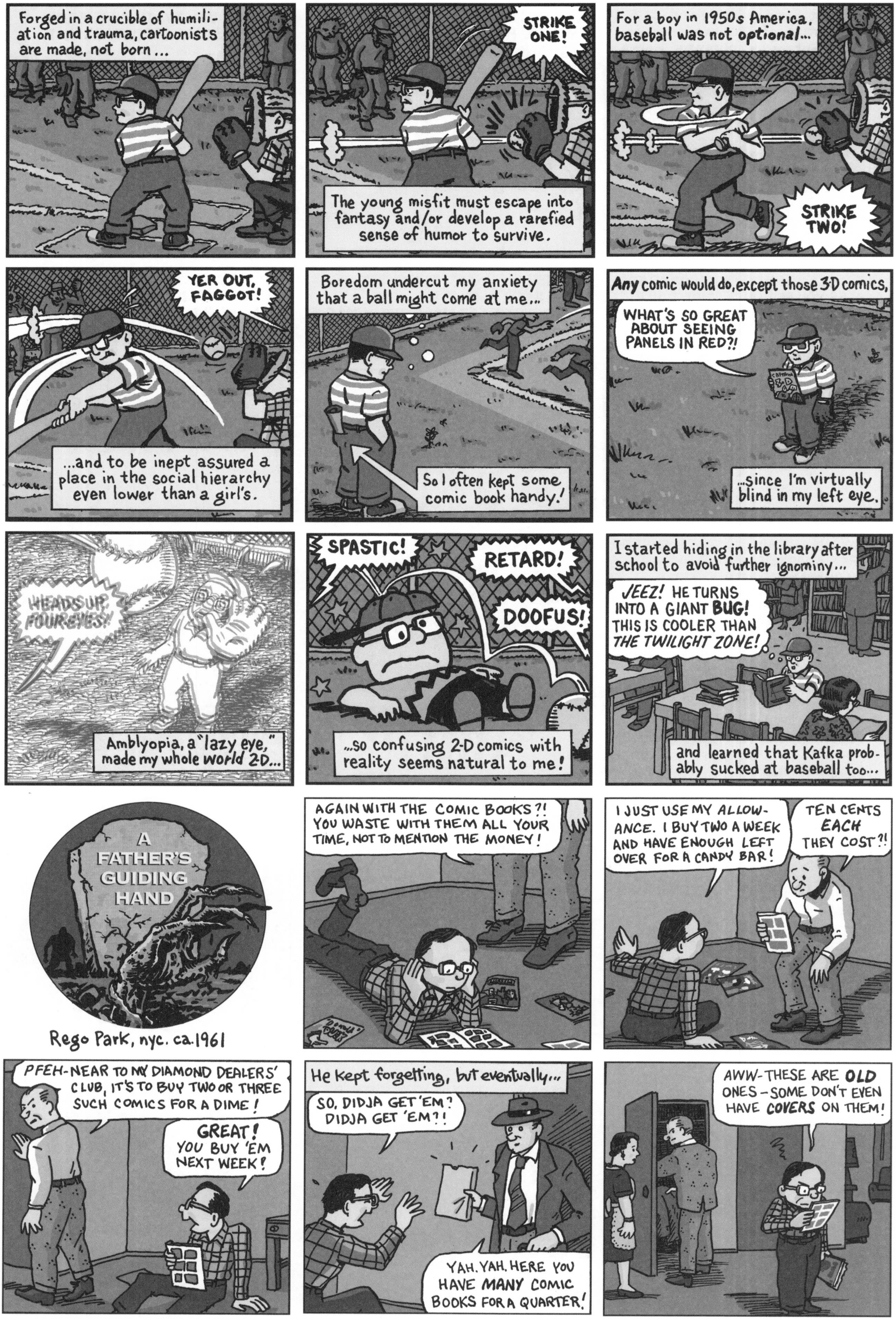
Forged in a crucible of humiliation and trauma, cartoonists are made, not born...
STRIKE ONE!
The young misfit must escape into fantasy and/or develop a rarefied sense of humor to survive.
For a boy in 1950s America, baseball was not optional...
STRIKE TWO!
YER OUT, FAGGOT!
...and to be inept assured a place in the social hierarchy even lower than a girl's.
Boredom undercut my anxiety that a ball might come at me...
So I often kept some comic book handy!
Any comic would do, except those 3-D comics,
WHAT'S SO GREAT ABOUT SEEING PANELS IN RED?!
...since I'm virtually blind in my left eye.
HEADS UP, FOUR-EYES!
Amblyopia, a "lazy eye," made my whole world 2-D...
SPASTIC!
RETARD!
DOOFUS!
...so confusing 2-D comics with reality seems natural to me!
I started hiding in the library after school to avoid further ignominy...
JEEZ! HE TURNS INTO A GIANT BUG! THIS IS COOLER THAN THE TWILIGHT ZONE!
and learned that Kafka probably sucked at baseball too...
A FATHER'S GUIDING HAND
Rego Park, nyc. ca. 1961
AGAIN WITH THE COMIC BOOKS?! YOU WASTE WITH THEM ALL YOUR TIME, NOT TO MENTION THE MONEY!
I JUST USE MY ALLOWANCE. I BUY TWO A WEEK AND HAVE ENOUGH LEFT OVER FOR A CANDY BAR!
TEN CENTS EACH THEY COST?!
PFEH- NEAR TO MY DIAMOND DEALERS' CLUB, IT'S TO BUY TWO OR THREE SUCH COMICS FOR A DIME!
GREAT! YOU BUY 'EM NEXT WEEK!
He kept forgetting, but eventually...
SO, DIDJA GET 'EM? DIDJA GET 'EM?!
YAH, YAH. HERE YOU HAVE MANY COMIC BOOKS FOR A QUARTER!
AWW- THESE ARE OLD ONES - SOME DON'T EVEN HAVE COVERS ON THEM!

But... **JEEZIS!** I had never seen comics like these before!

Six years earlier, Dr. Fredric Wertham had been as shocked by these comics as I was. Evidently they caused juvenile delinquency.

His crusade left only relatively insipid comics on the newsstands... the only ones I'd seen 'til my father intervened.

APPROVED BY THE COMICS CODE AUTHORITY

My father knew a lot about bargains... ...but *nothing* about the comic book burnings and the Senate hearings that put many comics publishers out of business.

I fell head over heels into a dangerous adult world of violent, sexually charged images!

HEY, POPS- THOSE COMICS YOU GOT ME WEREN'T *BAD!* HERE'S A QUARTER FOR NEXT WEEK'S BATCH!

...BUT NEXT TIME TRY NOT TO BUY ANY WITH "LOVE" OR "ROMANCE" IN THE TITLE!

Memory Hole

Soho, nyc. 2005

I TAILED THE LITTLE SQUIRT AS HE GOT LOST IN THE SQUALID LABYRINTHS OF HIS PAST.

HE KEPT DUCKING FROM ONE MEMORY TO ANOTHER TRYING TO LOCATE THE MOMENTS THAT SHAPED AND MISSHAPED HIM!

THE FETID SMELL OF HIS SELF-ABSORPTION MADE ME GAG, BUT I GOT CLOSER AND SNARLED: STOP WHINING, YA CRYBABY!

Li'l PITCHER

Washington Heights, nyc.
(a hired car ride home), ca. 1954

POP ART

Soho, nyc. ca. 2004

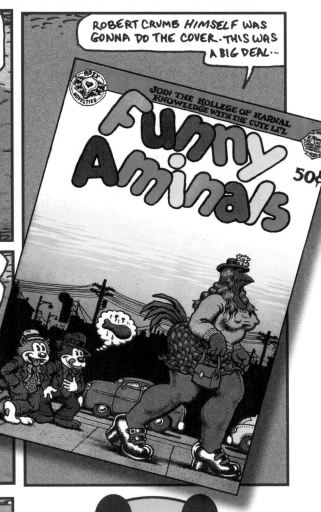

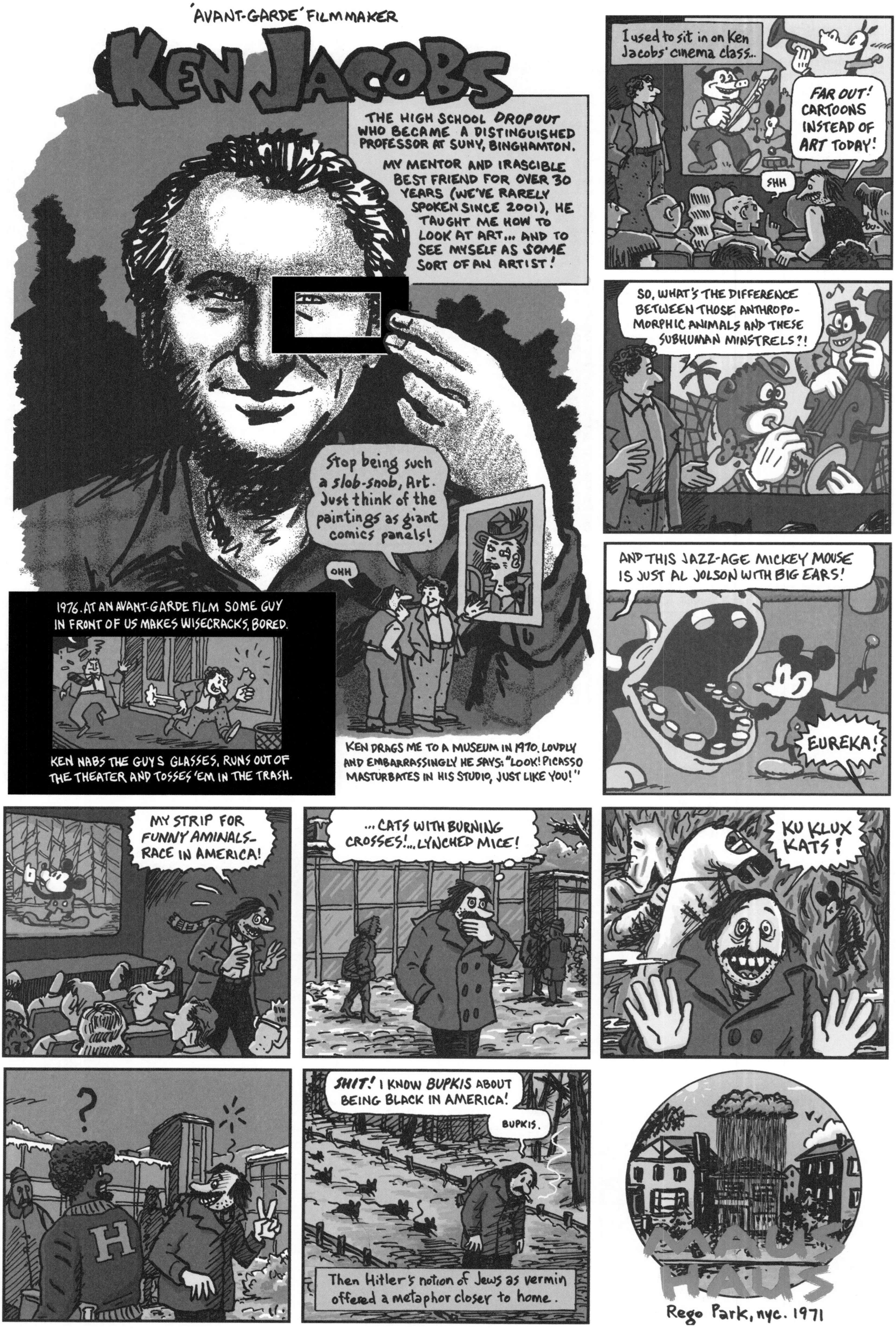

'AVANT-GARDE' FILMMAKER
KEN JACOBS
THE HIGH SCHOOL DROPOUT WHO BECAME A DISTINGUISHED PROFESSOR AT SUNY, BINGHAMTON.
MY MENTOR AND IRASCIBLE BEST FRIEND FOR OVER 30 YEARS (WE'VE RARELY SPOKEN SINCE 2001), HE TAUGHT ME HOW TO LOOK AT ART... AND TO SEE MYSELF AS SOME SORT OF AN ARTIST!
Stop being such a slob-snob, Art. Just think of the paintings as giant comics panels!
OHH
KEN DRAGS ME TO A MUSEUM IN 1970. LOUDLY AND EMBARRASSINGLY HE SAYS: "LOOK! PICASSO MASTURBATES IN HIS STUDIO, JUST LIKE YOU!"
1976. AT AN AVANT-GARDE FILM SOME GUY IN FRONT OF US MAKES WISECRACKS, BORED.
KEN NABS THE GUYS GLASSES, RUNS OUT OF THE THEATER AND TOSSES 'EM IN THE TRASH.
I used to sit in on Ken Jacobs' cinema class..
FAR OUT! CARTOONS INSTEAD OF ART TODAY!
SHH
SO, WHAT'S THE DIFFERENCE BETWEEN THOSE ANTHROPO-MORPHIC ANIMALS AND THESE SUBHUMAN MINSTRELS?!
AND THIS JAZZ-AGE MICKEY MOUSE IS JUST AL JOLSON WITH BIG EARS!
EUREKA!
MY STRIP FOR FUNNY AMINALS-RACE IN AMERICA!
...CATS WITH BURNING CROSSES!...LYNCHED MICE!
KU KLUX KATS!
?
SHIT! I KNOW BUPKIS ABOUT BEING BLACK IN AMERICA!
BUPKIS.
Then Hitler's notion of Jews as vermin offered a metaphor closer to home.
MAUS HAUS
Rego Park, nyc. 1971

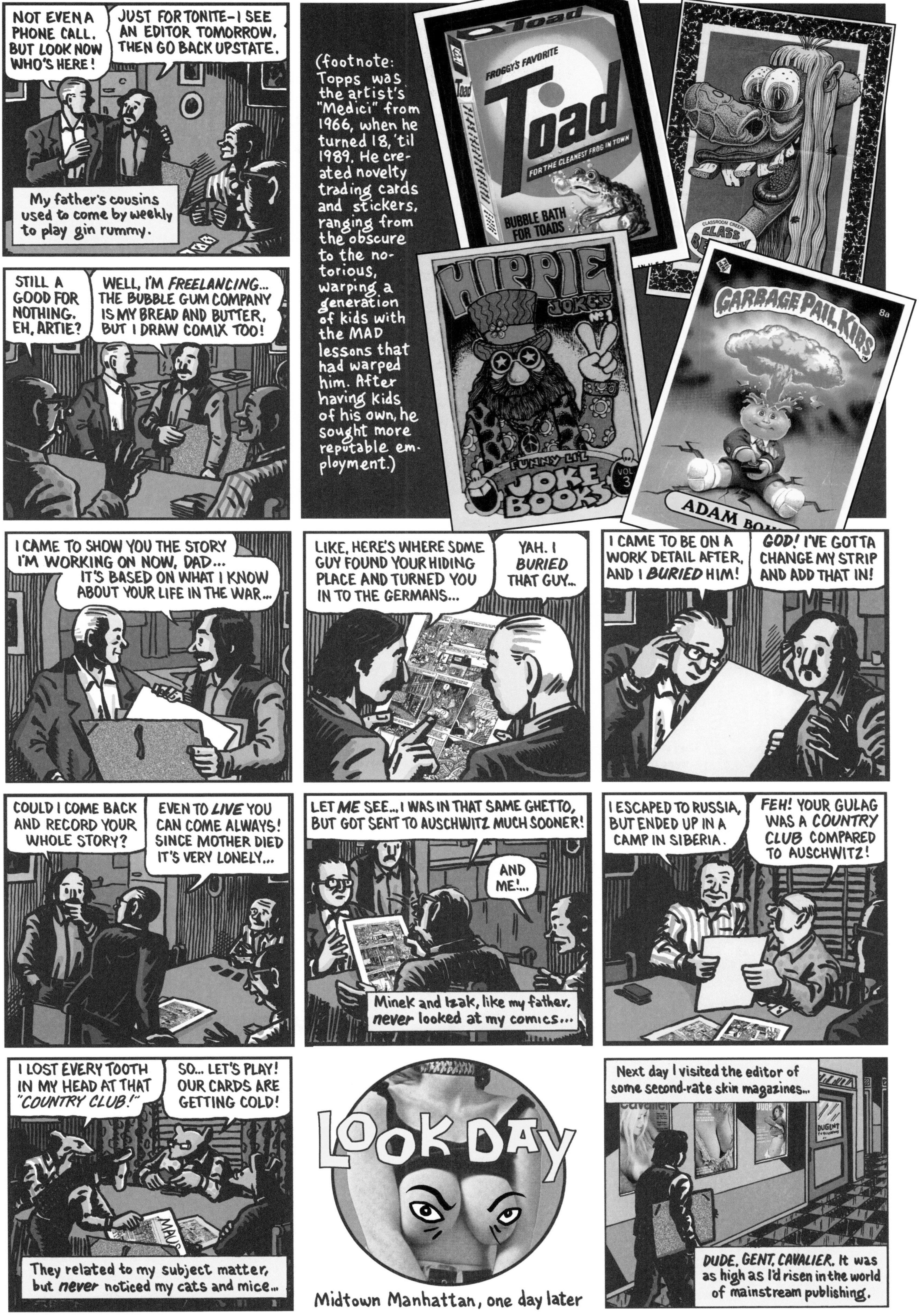
NOT EVEN A PHONE CALL. BUT LOOK NOW WHO'S HERE!
JUST FOR TONITE–I SEE AN EDITOR TOMORROW, THEN GO BACK UPSTATE.
My father's cousins used to come by weekly to play gin rummy.
STILL A GOOD FOR NOTHING. EH, ARTIE?
WELL, I'M FREELANCING... THE BUBBLE GUM COMPANY IS MY BREAD AND BUTTER, BUT I DRAW COMIX TOO!
(footnote: Topps was the artist's "Medici" from 1966, when he turned 18, 'til 1989. He created novelty trading cards and stickers, ranging from the obscure to the notorious, warping a generation of kids with the MAD lessons that had warped him. After having kids of his own, he sought more reputable employment.)
FROGGY'S FAVORITE
Toad
FOR THE CLEANEST FROG IN TOWN
BUBBLE BATH FOR TOADS
HIPPIE JOKES No 1
FUNNY LI'L JOKE BOOKS VOL 3
GARBAGE PAIL KIDS
8a
I CAME TO SHOW YOU THE STORY I'M WORKING ON NOW, DAD... IT'S BASED ON WHAT I KNOW ABOUT YOUR LIFE IN THE WAR...
LIKE, HERE'S WHERE SOME GUY FOUND YOUR HIDING PLACE AND TURNED YOU IN TO THE GERMANS...
YAH. I BURIED THAT GUY...
I CAME TO BE ON A WORK DETAIL AFTER, AND I BURIED HIM!
GOD! I'VE GOTTA CHANGE MY STRIP AND ADD THAT IN!
COULD I COME BACK AND RECORD YOUR WHOLE STORY?
EVEN TO LIVE YOU CAN COME ALWAYS! SINCE MOTHER DIED IT'S VERY LONELY...
LET ME SEE... I WAS IN THAT SAME GHETTO, BUT GOT SENT TO AUSCHWITZ MUCH SOONER!
AND ME!...
Minek and Izak, like my father, never looked at my comics...
I ESCAPED TO RUSSIA, BUT ENDED UP IN A CAMP IN SIBERIA.
FEH! YOUR GULAG WAS A COUNTRY CLUB COMPARED TO AUSCHWITZ!
I LOST EVERY TOOTH IN MY HEAD AT THAT "COUNTRY CLUB!"
SO... LET'S PLAY! OUR CARDS ARE GETTING COLD!
They related to my subject matter, but never noticed my cats and mice...
LOOK DAY
Midtown Manhattan, one day later
Next day I visited the editor of some second-rate skin magazines...
DUDE, GENT, CAVALIER. It was as high as I'd risen in the world of mainstream publishing.

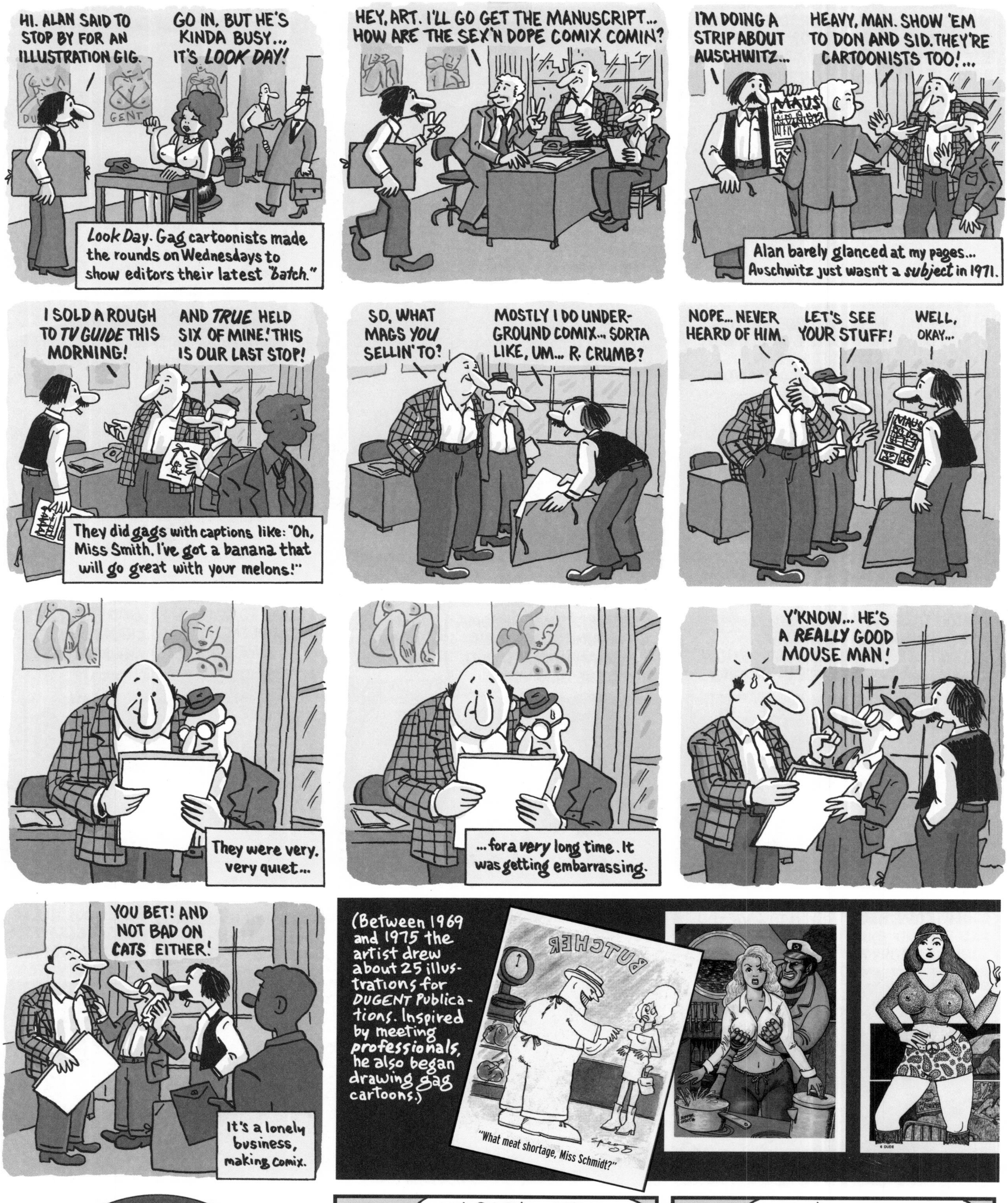
HI. ALAN SAID TO STOP BY FOR AN ILLUSTRATION GIG.
GO IN, BUT HE'S KINDA BUSY... IT'S LOOK DAY!
Look Day. Gag cartoonists made the rounds on Wednesdays to show editors their latest "batch."
HEY, ART. I'LL GO GET THE MANUSCRIPT... HOW ARE THE SEX'N DOPE COMIX COMIN?
I'M DOING A STRIP ABOUT AUSCHWITZ...
HEAVY, MAN. SHOW 'EM TO DON AND SID. THEY'RE CARTOONISTS TOO!...
Alan barely glanced at my pages... Auschwitz just wasn't a subject in 1971.
I SOLD A ROUGH TO TV GUIDE THIS MORNING!
AND TRUE HELD SIX OF MINE! THIS IS OUR LAST STOP!
They did gags with captions like: "Oh, Miss Smith, I've got a banana that will go great with your melons!"
SO, WHAT MAGS YOU SELLIN' TO?
MOSTLY I DO UNDERGROUND COMIX... SORTA LIKE, UM... R. CRUMB?
NOPE... NEVER HEARD OF HIM.
LET'S SEE YOUR STUFF!
WELL, OKAY...
They were very, very quiet...
...for a very long time. It was getting embarrassing.
Y'KNOW... HE'S A REALLY GOOD MOUSE MAN!
YOU BET! AND NOT BAD ON CATS EITHER!
It's a lonely business, making comix.
(Between 1969 and 1975 the artist drew about 25 illustrations for DUGENT Publications. Inspired by meeting professionals, he also began drawing gag cartoons.)
BUTCHER
"What meat shortage, Miss Schmidt?"

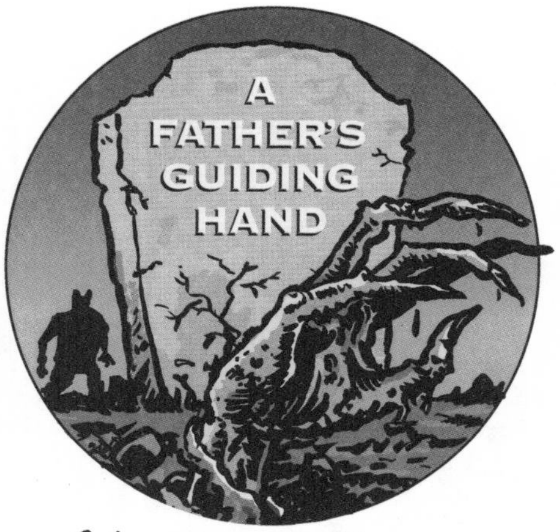
A FATHER'S GUIDING HAND

Soho, nyc. ca. 2004

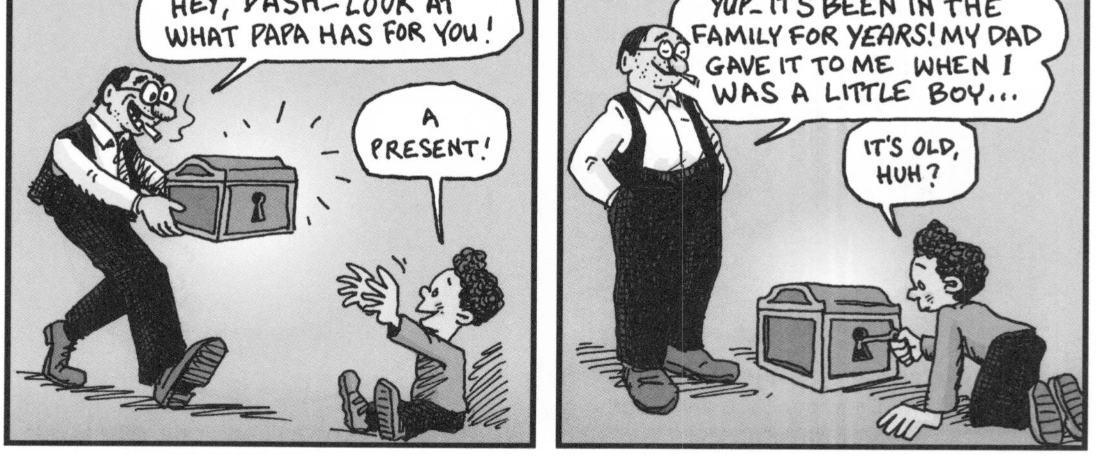
HEY, DASH- LOOK AT WHAT PAPA HAS FOR YOU!
A PRESENT!
YUP- IT'S BEEN IN THE FAMILY FOR YEARS! MY DAD GAVE IT TO ME WHEN I WAS A LITTLE BOY...
IT'S OLD, HUH?

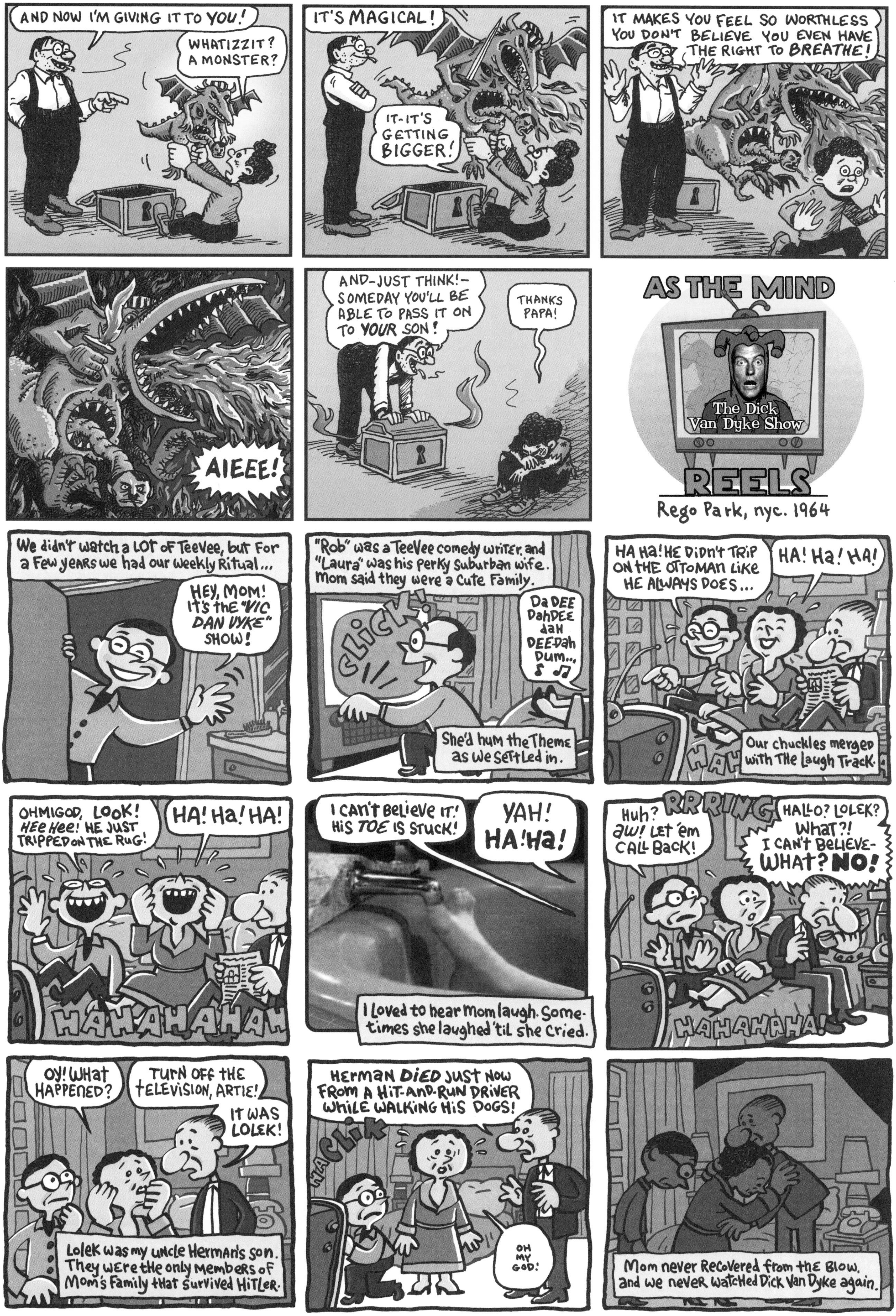
AND NOW I'M GIVING IT TO YOU!
WHATIZZIT? A MONSTER?
IT'S MAGICAL!
IT-IT'S GETTING BIGGER!
IT MAKES YOU FEEL SO WORTHLESS YOU DON'T BELIEVE YOU EVEN HAVE THE RIGHT TO BREATHE!
AIEEE!
AND–JUST THINK!– SOMEDAY YOU'LL BE ABLE TO PASS IT ON TO YOUR SON!
THANKS PAPA!
AS THE MIND REELS
The Dick Van Dyke Show
Rego Park, nyc. 1964
We didn't watch a LOT of TeeVee, but For a Few years we had our weekly Ritual...
HEY, MOM! IT'S the "VIC DAN VYKE" SHOW!
"Rob" was a TeeVee comedy writer, and "Laura" was his perky suburban wife. Mom said they were a Cute Family.
CLICK!
Da DEE DahDEE dah DEE-Dah Dum...
She'd hum the Theme as we settled in.
HA Ha! HE DIDN'T TRIP ON THE OTTOMAN LIKE HE ALWAYS DOES...
HA! Ha! HA!
HAH
Our chuckles merged with the Laugh Track.
OHMIGOD, LOOK! HEE Hee! HE JUST TRIPPED ON THE RUG!
HA! Ha! HA!
HAHAHAHAH
I CAN'T BELIEVE IT! HIS TOE IS STUCK!
YAH! HA! Ha!
I loved to hear Mom laugh. Sometimes she laughed 'til she cried.
RRRING
Huh? aw! Let 'em CALL Back!
HALLO? LOLEK? WHAT?! I CAN'T BELIEVE- WHAT? NO!
HAHAHAHA!
Oy! What HAPPENED?
TURN OFF THE TELEVISION, ARTIE!
IT WAS LOLEK!
Lolek was my uncle Herman's son. They were the only members of Mom's Family that survived Hitler.
HERMAN DIED JUST NOW FROM A HIT-AND-RUN DRIVER WHILE WALKING HIS DOGS!
HA CLIK
OH MY GOD!
Mom never Recovered from the Blow, and we never watched Dick Van Dyke again.

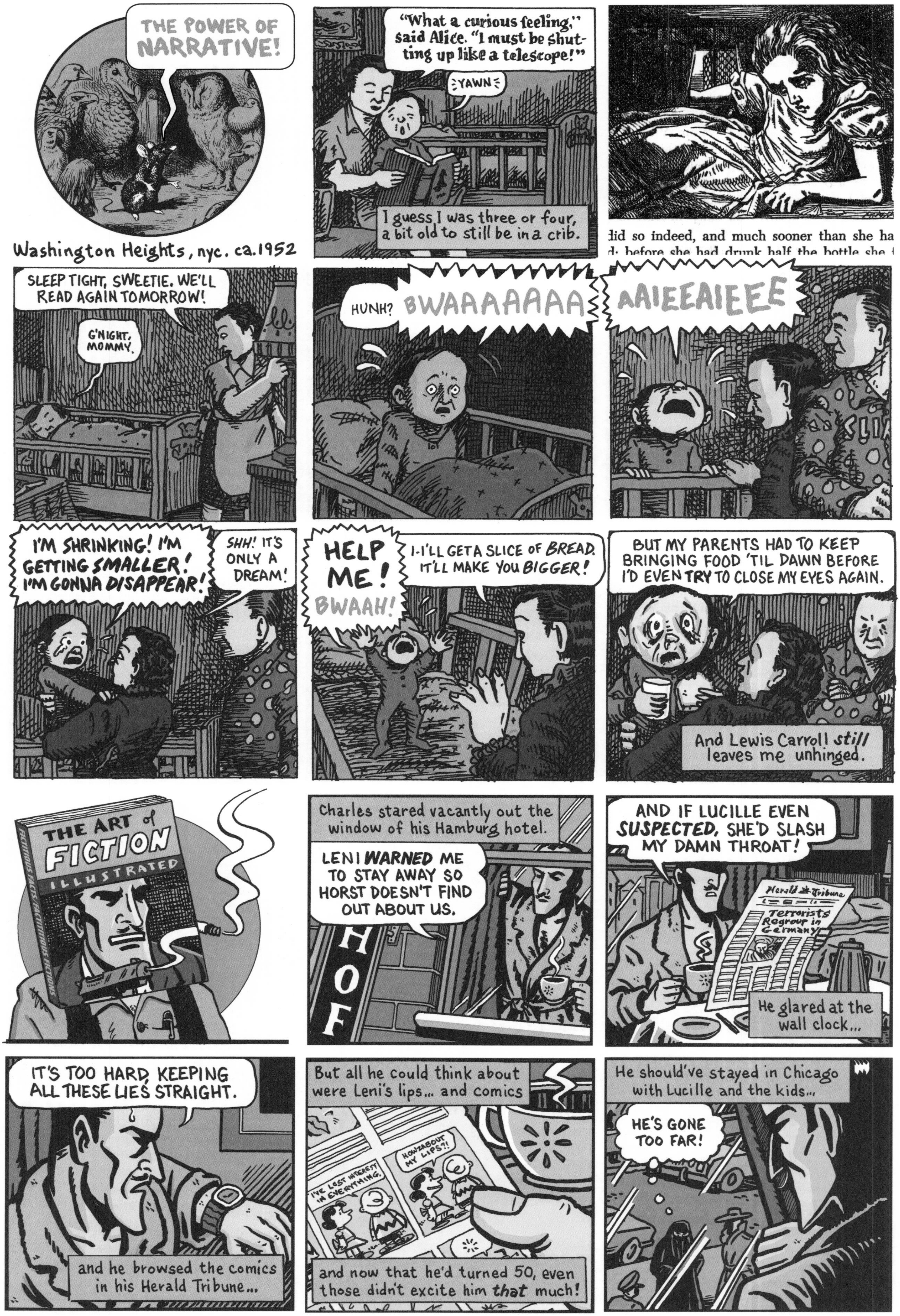
THE POWER OF NARRATIVE!
Washington Heights, nyc. ca.1952
"What a curious feeling," said Alice. "I must be shutting up like a telescope!"
YAWN
I guess I was three or four, a bit old to still be in a crib.
lid so indeed, and much sooner than she ha
SLEEP TIGHT, SWEETIE. WE'LL READ AGAIN TOMORROW!
G'NIGHT, MOMMY.
HUNH?
BWAAAAAAA
AAIEEAIEEE
I'M SHRINKING! I'M GETTING SMALLER! I'M GONNA DISAPPEAR!
SHH! IT'S ONLY A DREAM!
HELP ME! BWAAH!
I-I'LL GET A SLICE OF BREAD. IT'LL MAKE YOU BIGGER!
BUT MY PARENTS HAD TO KEEP BRINGING FOOD 'TIL DAWN BEFORE I'D EVEN TRY TO CLOSE MY EYES AGAIN.
And Lewis Carroll still leaves me unhinged.
THE ART of FICTION ILLUSTRATED
FICTITIOUS FACTS - FACTITIOUS FICTIONS
Charles stared vacantly out the window of his Hamburg hotel.
LENI WARNED ME TO STAY AWAY SO HORST DOESN'T FIND OUT ABOUT US.
HOF
AND IF LUCILLE EVEN SUSPECTED, SHE'D SLASH MY DAMN THROAT!
Herald Tribune
Terrorists Regroup in Germany
He glared at the wall clock...
IT'S TOO HARD KEEPING ALL THESE LIES STRAIGHT.
and he browsed the comics in his Herald Tribune...
But all he could think about were Leni's lips... and comics
I'VE LOST INTEREST IN EVERYTHING.
HOWZABOUT MY LIPS?!
and now that he'd turned 50, even those didn't excite him that much!
He should've stayed in Chicago with Lucille and the kids...
HE'S GONE TOO FAR!

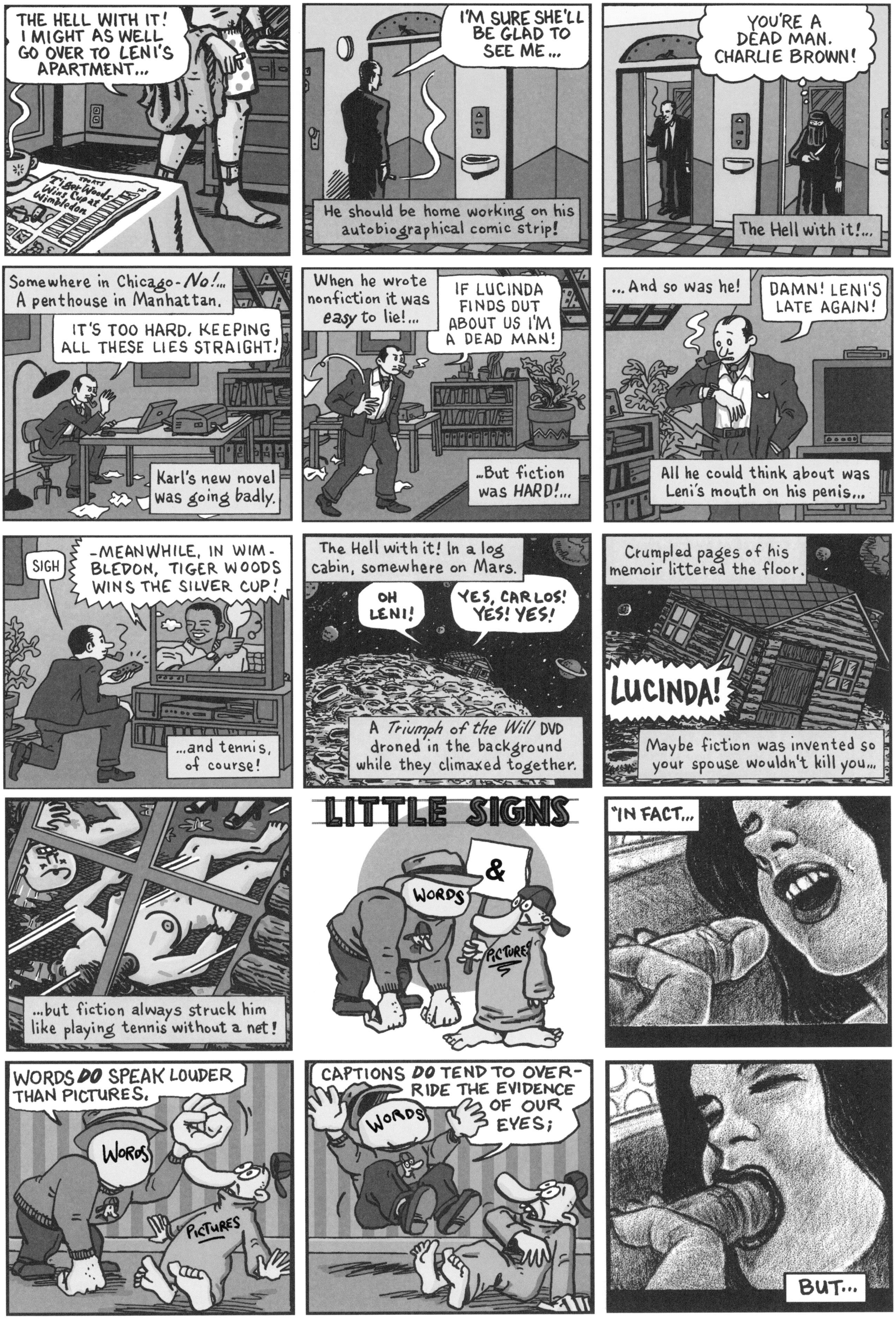
THE HELL WITH IT! I MIGHT AS WELL GO OVER TO LENI'S APARTMENT...
SPORTS Tiger Woods Wins Cup at Wimbledon
I'M SURE SHE'LL BE GLAD TO SEE ME...
He should be home working on his autobiographical comic strip!
YOU'RE A DEAD MAN. CHARLIE BROWN!
The Hell with it!...
Somewhere in Chicago-No!... A penthouse in Manhattan.
IT'S TOO HARD, KEEPING ALL THESE LIES STRAIGHT!
Karl's new novel was going badly.
When he wrote nonfiction it was easy to lie!...
IF LUCINDA FINDS OUT ABOUT US I'M A DEAD MAN!
...But fiction was HARD!...
...And so was he!
DAMN! LENI'S LATE AGAIN!
All he could think about was Leni's mouth on his penis...
SIGH
-MEANWHILE, IN WIMBLEDON, TIGER WOODS WINS THE SILVER CUP!
...and tennis, of course!
The Hell with it! In a log cabin, somewhere on Mars.
OH LENI!
YES, CARLOS! YES! YES!
A Triumph of the Will DVD droned in the background while they climaxed together.
Crumpled pages of his memoir littered the floor.
LUCINDA!
Maybe fiction was invented so your spouse wouldn't kill you...
...but fiction always struck him like playing tennis without a net!
LITTLE SIGNS
&
WORDS
PICTURES
"IN FACT...
WORDS DO SPEAK LOUDER THAN PICTURES,
WORDS
PICTURES
CAPTIONS DO TEND TO OVERRIDE THE EVIDENCE OF OUR EYES;
WORDS
BUT...

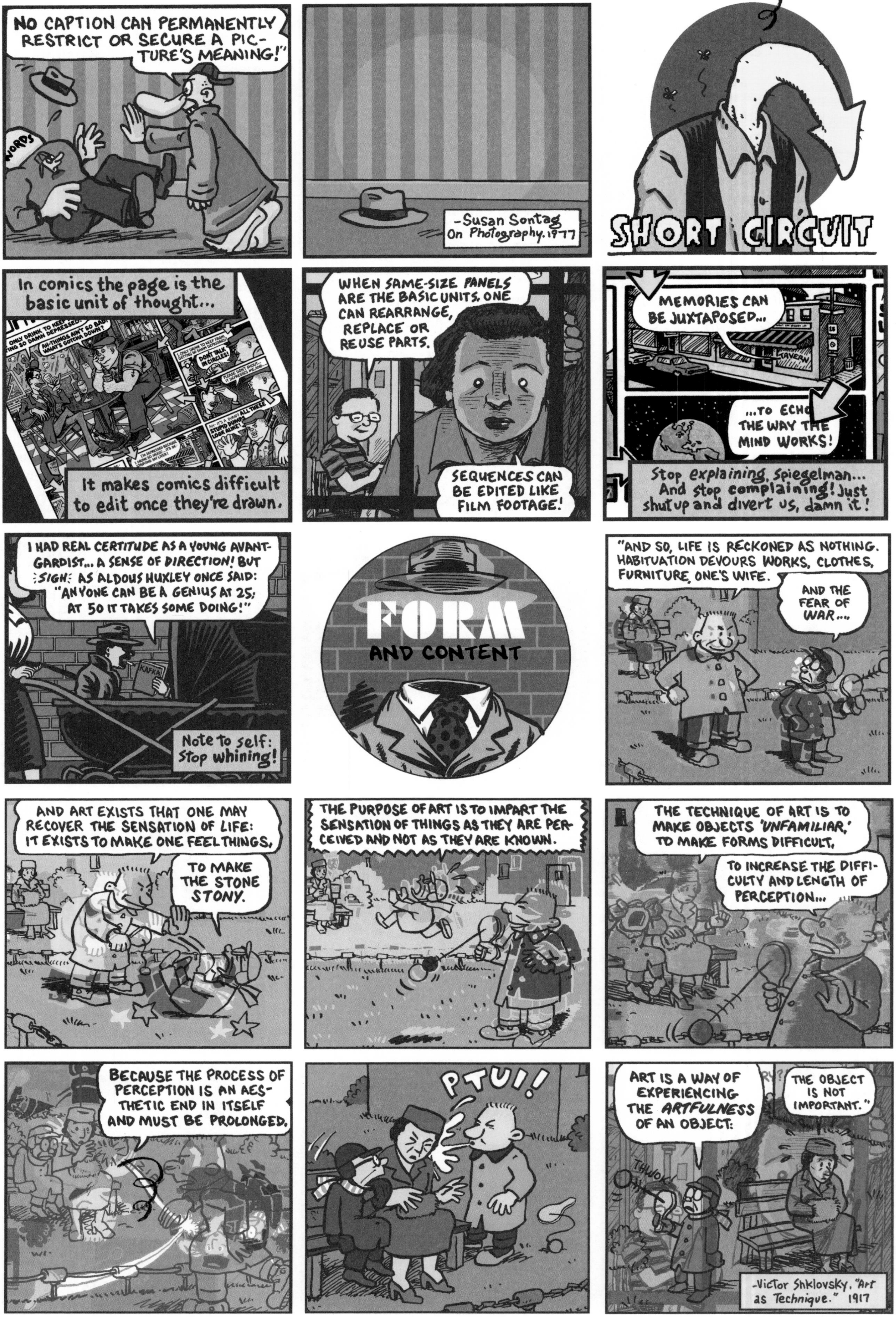

NO CAPTION CAN PERMANENTLY RESTRICT OR SECURE A PICTURE'S MEANING!"
WORDS
-Susan Sontag On Photography. 1977
SHORT CIRCUIT
In comics the page is the basic unit of thought...
It makes comics difficult to edit once they're drawn.
WHEN SAME-SIZE PANELS ARE THE BASIC UNITS, ONE CAN REARRANGE, REPLACE OR REUSE PARTS.
SEQUENCES CAN BE EDITED LIKE FILM FOOTAGE!
MEMORIES CAN BE JUXTAPOSED...
...TO ECHO THE WAY THE MIND WORKS!
Stop explaining, Spiegelman... And stop complaining! Just shut up and divert us, damn it!
I HAD REAL CERTITUDE AS A YOUNG AVANT-GARDIST... A SENSE OF DIRECTION! BUT :SIGH: AS ALDOUS HUXLEY ONCE SAID: "ANYONE CAN BE A GENIUS AT 25; AT 50 IT TAKES SOME DOING!"
KAFKA
Note to self: Stop whining!
FORM AND CONTENT
"AND SO, LIFE IS RECKONED AS NOTHING. HABITUATION DEVOURS WORKS, CLOTHES, FURNITURE, ONE'S WIFE.
AND THE FEAR OF WAR....
AND ART EXISTS THAT ONE MAY RECOVER THE SENSATION OF LIFE: IT EXISTS TO MAKE ONE FEEL THINGS,
TO MAKE THE STONE STONY.
THE PURPOSE OF ART IS TO IMPART THE SENSATION OF THINGS AS THEY ARE PERCEIVED AND NOT AS THEY ARE KNOWN.
THE TECHNIQUE OF ART IS TO MAKE OBJECTS 'UNFAMILIAR,' TO MAKE FORMS DIFFICULT,
TO INCREASE THE DIFFICULTY AND LENGTH OF PERCEPTION...
BECAUSE THE PROCESS OF PERCEPTION IS AN AESTHETIC END IN ITSELF AND MUST BE PROLONGED.
PTUI!
ART IS A WAY OF EXPERIENCING THE ARTFULNESS OF AN OBJECT:
THE OBJECT IS NOT IMPORTANT."
THWOK!
-Victor Shklovsky, "Art as Technique." 1917

art spiegelman

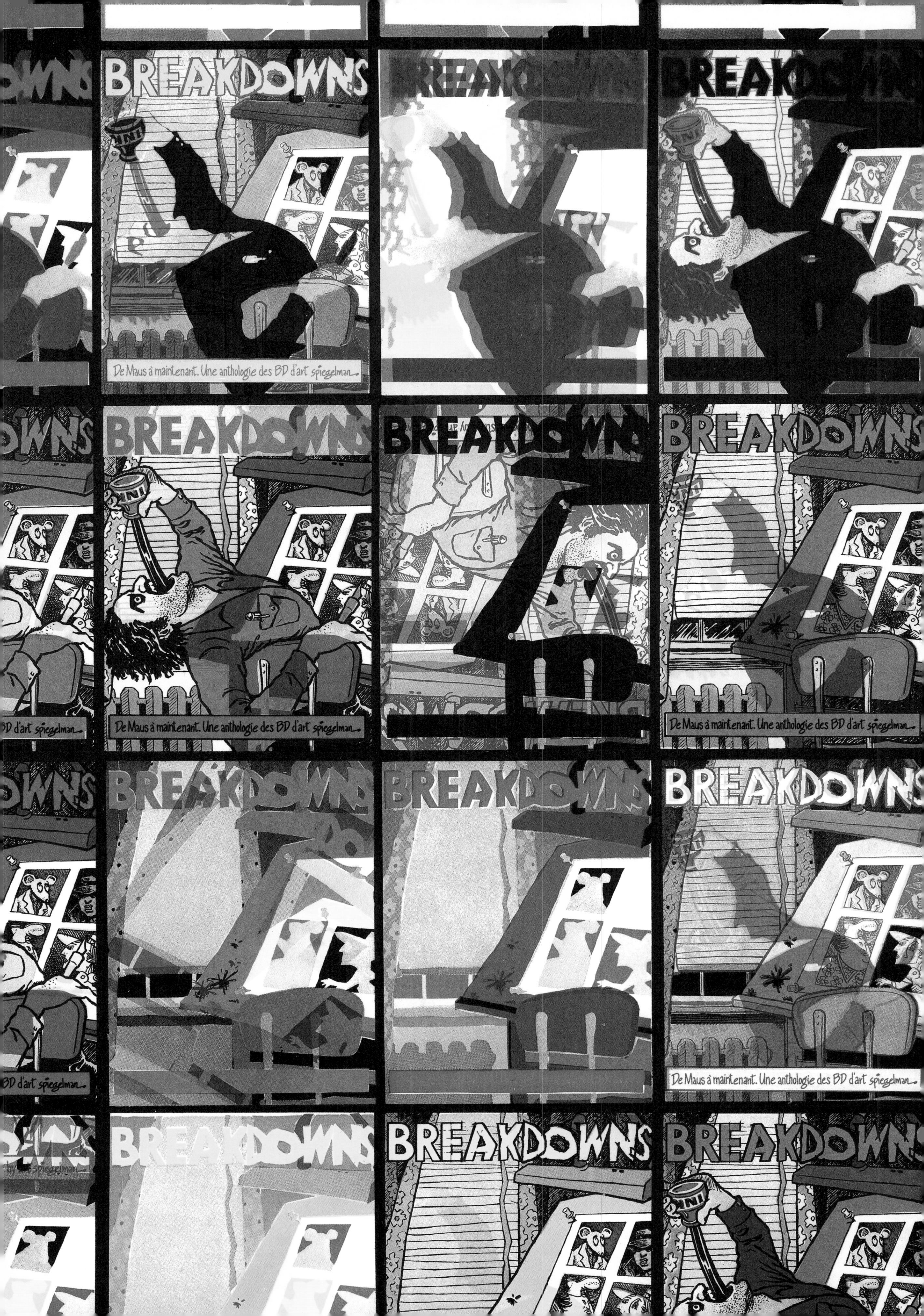
BREAKDOWNS
De Maus à maintenant. Une anthologie des BD d'art spiegelman
BREAKDOWNS
BREAKDOWNS
BREAKDOWNS
BREAKDOWNS
De Maus à maintenant. Une anthologie des BD d'art spiegelman
BREAKDOWNS
De Maus à maintenant. Une anthologie des BD d'art spiegelman
BREAKDOWNS
BREAKDOWNS
BREAKDOWNS
De Maus à maintenant. Une anthologie des BD d'art spiegelman
BREAKDOWNS
BREAKDOWNS
BREAKDOWNS

DON'T BELIEVE EVERYTHING YOU READ!...

The publishing information on the following two pages is *incorrect*.

This book is *not* published by NOSTALGIA PRESS.

(Therein hangs a tale, one better left untold. Just let it be known that this book could not have been more aptly named...)

BREAKDOWNS. Published by:

BÉLIER PRESS
P.O. BOX 'C'
GRACIE STATION
NEW YORK, N.Y. 10028

(Additional copies available from Bélier Press for $8.95 post paid.)

International Standard Book Number: 0-914646-14-1

Library of Congress Catalogue Card Number: 77-93591

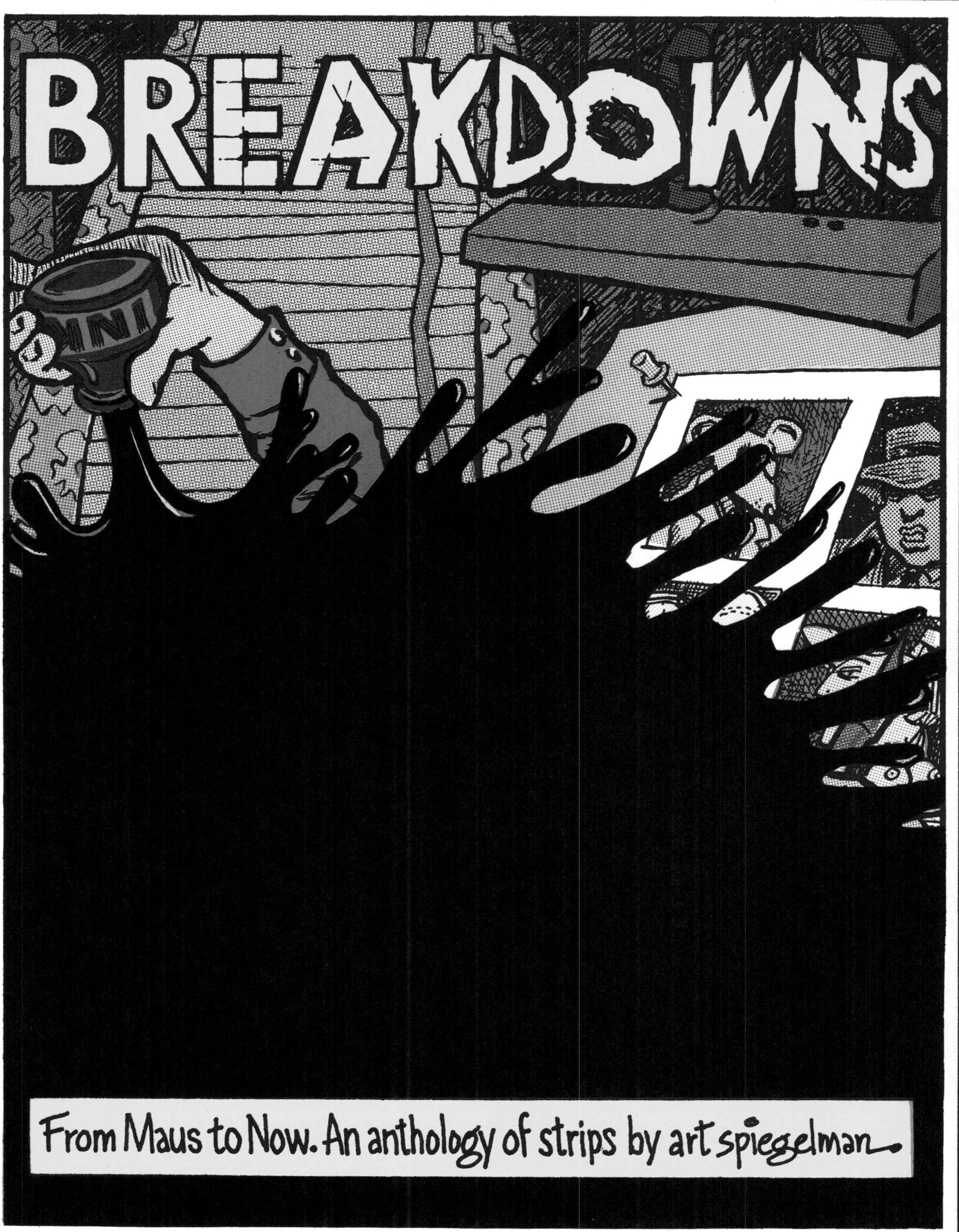
BREAKDOWNS
INI
From Maus to Now. An anthology of strips by art spiegelman

NOSTALGIA PRESS INC. NEW YORK

International Standard Book Number: 0-87897-052-5

First printing: December 1977
Printed in the United States of America.

Published by Nostalgia Press Inc., Box 293, Franklin Sq., New York. 11010
Additional copies available from the Publisher for $ 8.95, post paid.

Printed by Quad Offset Corporation, 250 Hudson St., N.Y.C., N.Y. 10013.
Bound by Publishers Book Bindery, Inc., Long Island City, N.Y. 11101.

INTRO

My dictionary defines COMIC STRIP as "a narrative series of cartoons."

A NARRATIVE is defined as "a story." Most definitions of STORY leave me cold.

Except the one that says: "A complete horizontal division of a building... [From Medieval Latin HISTORIA... a row of windows with pictures on them.]"

The word CARTOONS implies humorous intent - a desire to amuse and entertain.

I'm not *necessarily* interested in entertainment - in creating diversions.

Better than CARTOONS is the word DRAWINGS; or better still...DIAGRAMS.

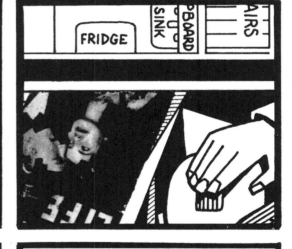

"It is up to the careful comic artist to see that he offends no one, hurts no group and that his strip is all in good clean fun..."

"...All in all, drawing comic strips is very interesting..."

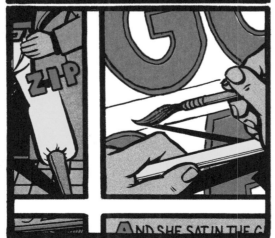

"...in a dull, monotonous sort of way."
—Chic Young, creator of BLONDIE

— art spiegelman — new york city. 1977

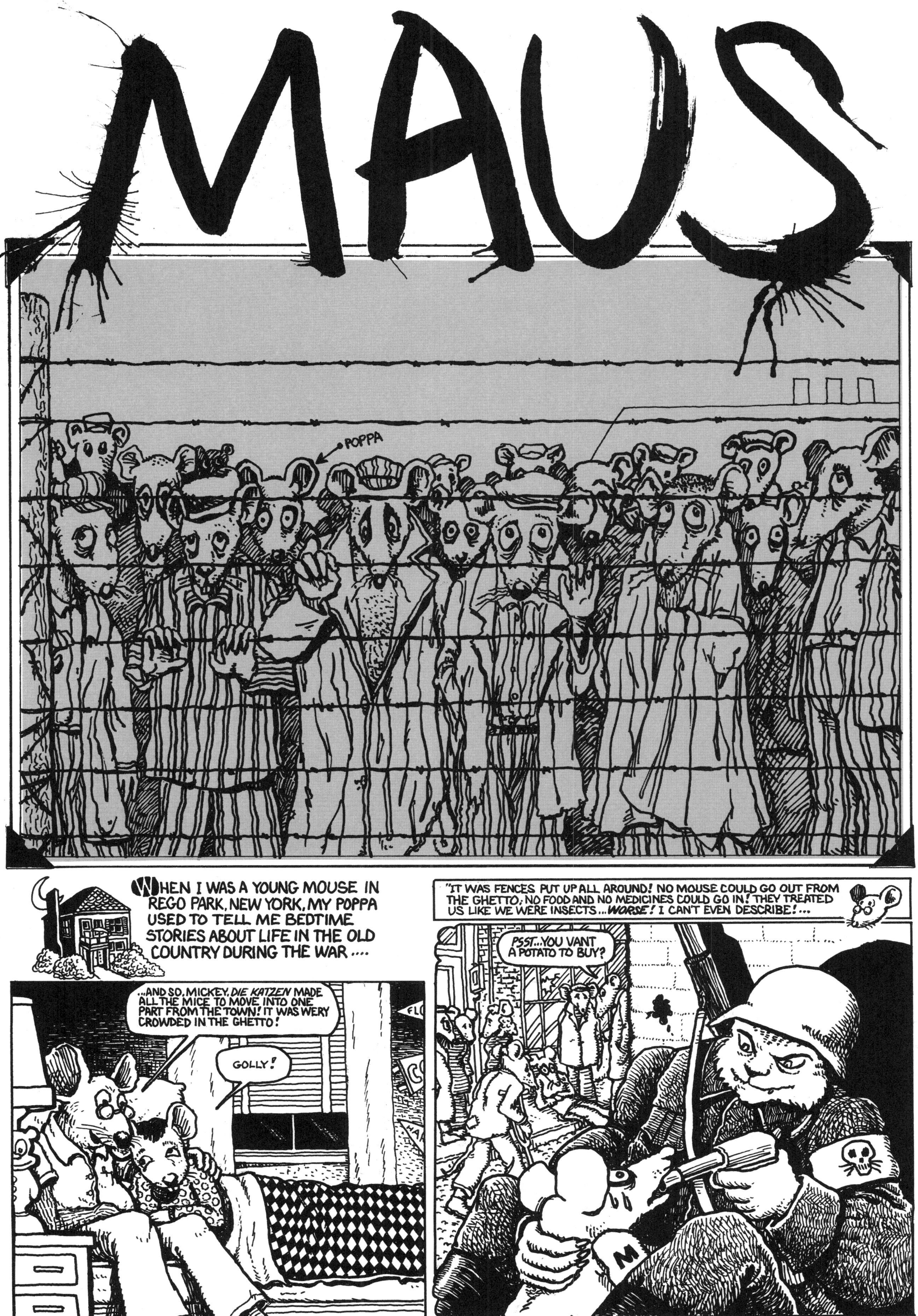
MAUS
POPPA
WHEN I WAS A YOUNG MOUSE IN REGO PARK, NEW YORK, MY POPPA USED TO TELL ME BEDTIME STORIES ABOUT LIFE IN THE OLD COUNTRY DURING THE WAR....
...AND SO, MICKEY, *DIE KATZEN* MADE ALL THE MICE TO MOVE INTO ONE PART FROM THE TOWN! IT WAS WERY CROWDED IN THE GHETTO!
GOLLY!
"IT WAS FENCES PUT UP ALL AROUND! NO MOUSE COULD GO OUT FROM THE GHETTO; NO FOOD AND NO MEDICINES COULD GO IN! THEY TREATED US LIKE WE WERE INSECTS... *WORSE!* I CAN'T EVEN DESCRIBE!...
PSST...YOU VANT A POTATO TO BUY?
M
©1972 art spiegelman

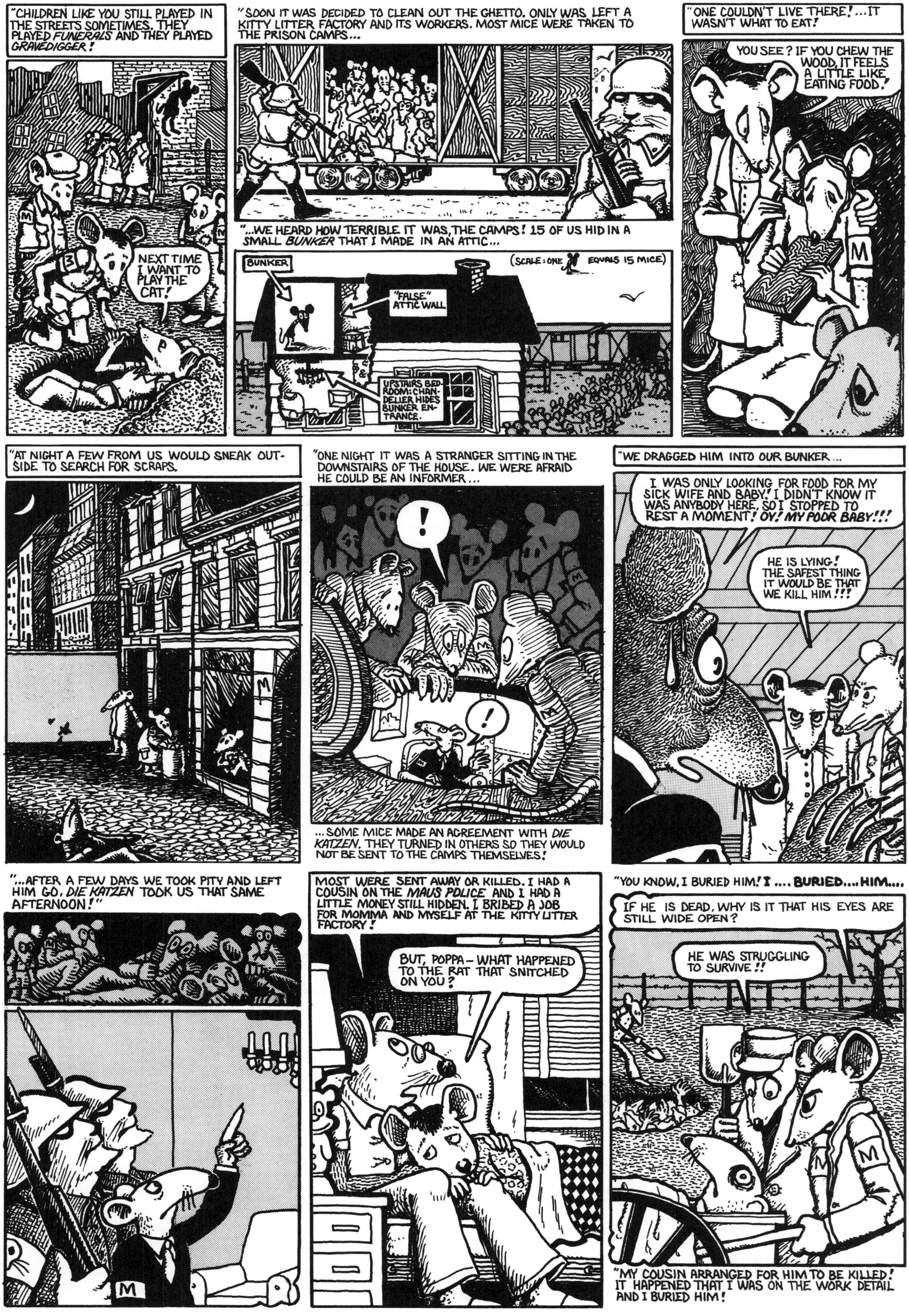
"CHILDREN LIKE YOU STILL PLAYED IN THE STREETS SOMETIMES. THEY PLAYED *FUNERALS* AND THEY PLAYED *GRAVEDIGGER*!
NEXT TIME I WANT TO PLAY THE CAT!
"SOON IT WAS DECIDED TO CLEAN OUT THE GHETTO. ONLY WAS LEFT A KITTY LITTER FACTORY AND ITS WORKERS. MOST MICE WERE TAKEN TO THE PRISON CAMPS...
"...WE HEARD HOW TERRIBLE IT WAS, THE CAMPS! 15 OF US HID IN A SMALL *BUNKER* THAT I MADE IN AN ATTIC...
(SCALE: ONE EQUALS 15 MICE)
BUNKER
"FALSE" ATTIC WALL
UPSTAIRS BEDROOM: CHANDELIER HIDES BUNKER ENTRANCE.
"ONE COULDN'T LIVE THERE!...IT WASN'T WHAT TO EAT!
YOU SEE? IF YOU CHEW THE WOOD, IT FEELS A LITTLE LIKE EATING FOOD!
"AT NIGHT A FEW FROM US WOULD SNEAK OUTSIDE TO SEARCH FOR SCRAPS.
"ONE NIGHT IT WAS A STRANGER SITTING IN THE DOWNSTAIRS OF THE HOUSE. WE WERE AFRAID HE COULD BE AN INFORMER...
!
!
...SOME MICE MADE AN AGREEMENT WITH *DIE KATZEN*. THEY TURNED IN OTHERS SO THEY WOULD NOT BE SENT TO THE CAMPS THEMSELVES!
"WE DRAGGED HIM INTO OUR BUNKER...
I WAS ONLY LOOKING FOR FOOD FOR MY SICK WIFE AND BABY! I DIDN'T KNOW IT WAS ANYBODY HERE, SO I STOPPED TO REST A MOMENT! *OY! MY POOR BABY!!!*
HE IS LYING! THE SAFEST THING IT WOULD BE THAT WE KILL HIM!!!
"...AFTER A FEW DAYS WE TOOK PITY AND LEFT HIM GO. *DIE KATZEN* TOOK US THAT SAME AFTERNOON!"
MOST WERE SENT AWAY OR KILLED. I HAD A COUSIN ON THE *MAUS POLICE* AND I HAD A LITTLE MONEY STILL HIDDEN. I BRIBED A JOB FOR MOMMA AND MYSELF AT THE KITTY LITTER FACTORY!
BUT, POPPA – WHAT HAPPENED TO THE RAT THAT SNITCHED ON YOU?
"YOU KNOW, I BURIED HIM! **I .... BURIED.... HIM....**
IF HE IS DEAD, WHY IS IT THAT HIS EYES ARE STILL WIDE OPEN?
HE WAS STRUGGLING TO SURVIVE!!
"MY COUSIN ARRANGED FOR HIM TO BE KILLED! IT HAPPENED THAT I WAS ON THE WORK DETAIL AND I BURIED HIM!

"SO...IN TIME THE FACTORY WAS LIQUIDATED TOO, AND THE WHOLE GHETTO WAS CLOSED! AGAIN SOME FROM US MANAGED TO HIDE IN A CORNER..."

"DIE KATZEN MADE GUARDS AROUND TO STARVE OUT THOSE LEFT IN THE GHETTO..."

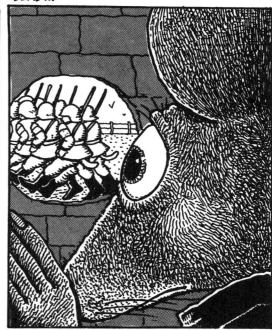

"AFTER SOME WEEKS THE GUARDS LEFT US FOR DEAD..."

...WE SAW THIS FROM A TINY HOLE THAT WE MADE IN THE WALL WITH A SMALL PIECE WOOD AND OUR NAILS!

"THERE WAS NO FOOD AT ALL! WE LEFT THE BUNKER, BUT WHERE TO GO? WHERE TO GO?..."

"WITH MY LAST MONEY I MADE A DEAL WITH ONE CAT TO SNEAK US OUT FROM THE COUNTRY..."

OKAY, MEET ME HERE TOMORROW MORNING! I'LL HIDE YOU IN MY WAGON!

THANK YOU, THANK YOU!

"THE NEXT MORNING WAS ONLY WAITING DIE KATZEN!..."

...THEY SENT US TO MAUSCHWITZ....

"YOUR MOMMA AND I SNEAKED TO HER OLD HOME TOWN....LOCAL CATS SHE KNEW BEFORE THE WAR WERE AFRAID TO HIDE US!"

GO AWAY! QUICKLY!!!

"... MAUSCHWITZ ... "

...AND SO IT WAS....I CAN TELL YOU NO MORE NOW....

"..I CAN TELL YOU NO MORE .... IT'S TIME TO GO TO SLEEP, MICKEY!"

UH-HUH... G'NIGHT, POPPA!

Zip·a·Tunes
and Moiré Melodies
featuring
SKEETER GRANT'S
SKINLESS PERKINS
*MOIRÉ (MÒ-RAY): A wavy, rippled pattern.
A "SOMERSAULT" FOR YOUR AMUSEMENT!
D-D-Dot's all, folks!
Zip·a·Tunes
© art spiegelman 1972

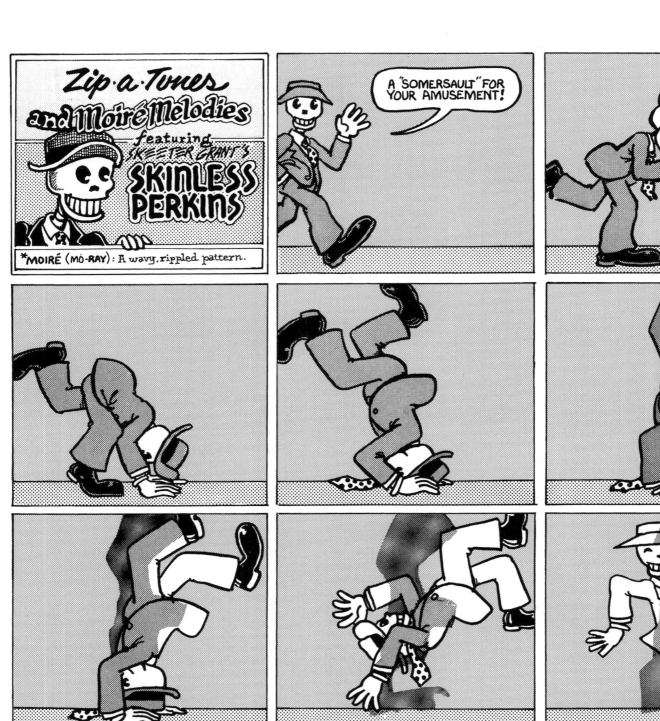

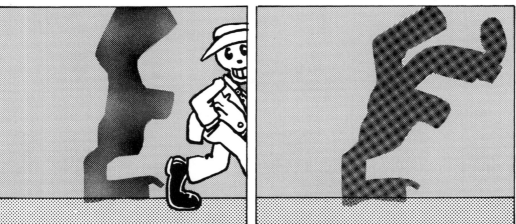

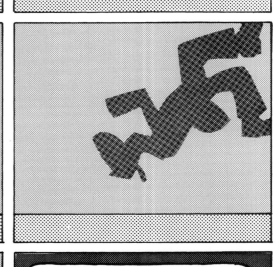

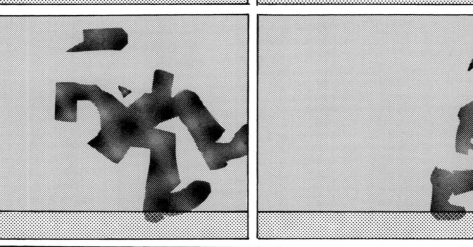

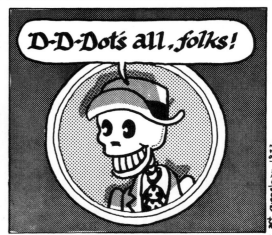

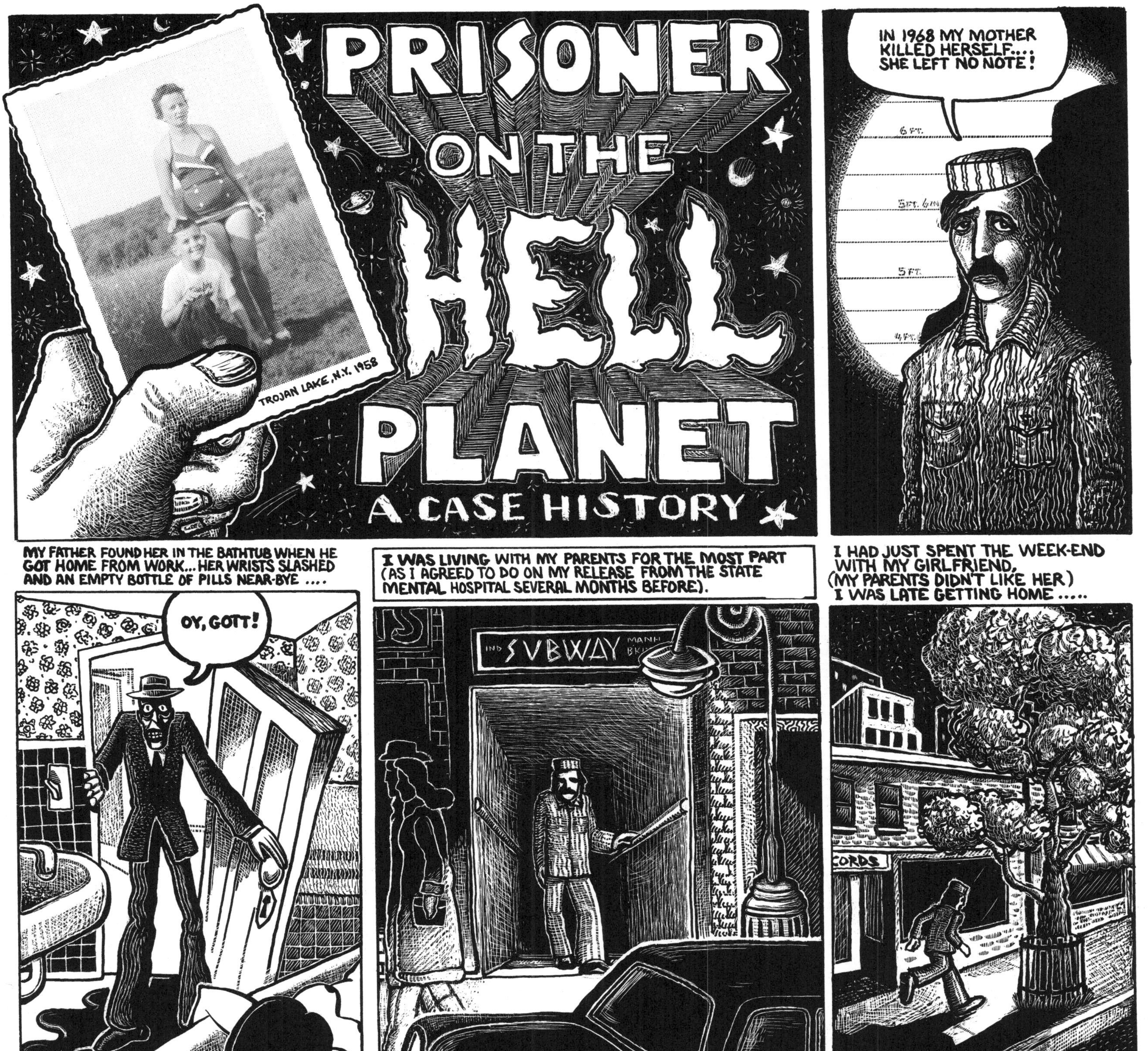
PRISONER ON THE HELL PLANET
A CASE HISTORY
TROJAN LAKE, N.Y. 1958
IN 1968 MY MOTHER KILLED HERSELF.... SHE LEFT NO NOTE!
MY FATHER FOUND HER IN THE BATHTUB WHEN HE GOT HOME FROM WORK... HER WRISTS SLASHED AND AN EMPTY BOTTLE OF PILLS NEAR-BYE ....
OY, GOTT!
I WAS LIVING WITH MY PARENTS FOR THE MOST PART (AS I AGREED TO DO ON MY RELEASE FROM THE STATE MENTAL HOSPITAL SEVERAL MONTHS BEFORE).
SUBWAY
I HAD JUST SPENT THE WEEK-END WITH MY GIRLFRIEND, (MY PARENTS DIDN'T LIKE HER) I WAS LATE GETTING HOME .....
CORDS
I SUPPOSE THAT IF I'D GOTTEN HOME WHEN EXPECTED, I WOULD HAVE FOUND HER BODY....
63-12
WHEN I SAW THE CROWD I HAD A PANG OF FEAR... I SUSPECTED THE WORST, BUT I DIDN'T LET MYSELF KNOW!

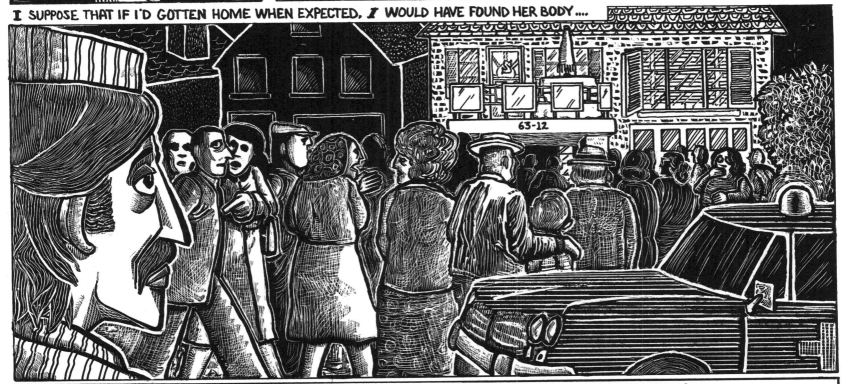

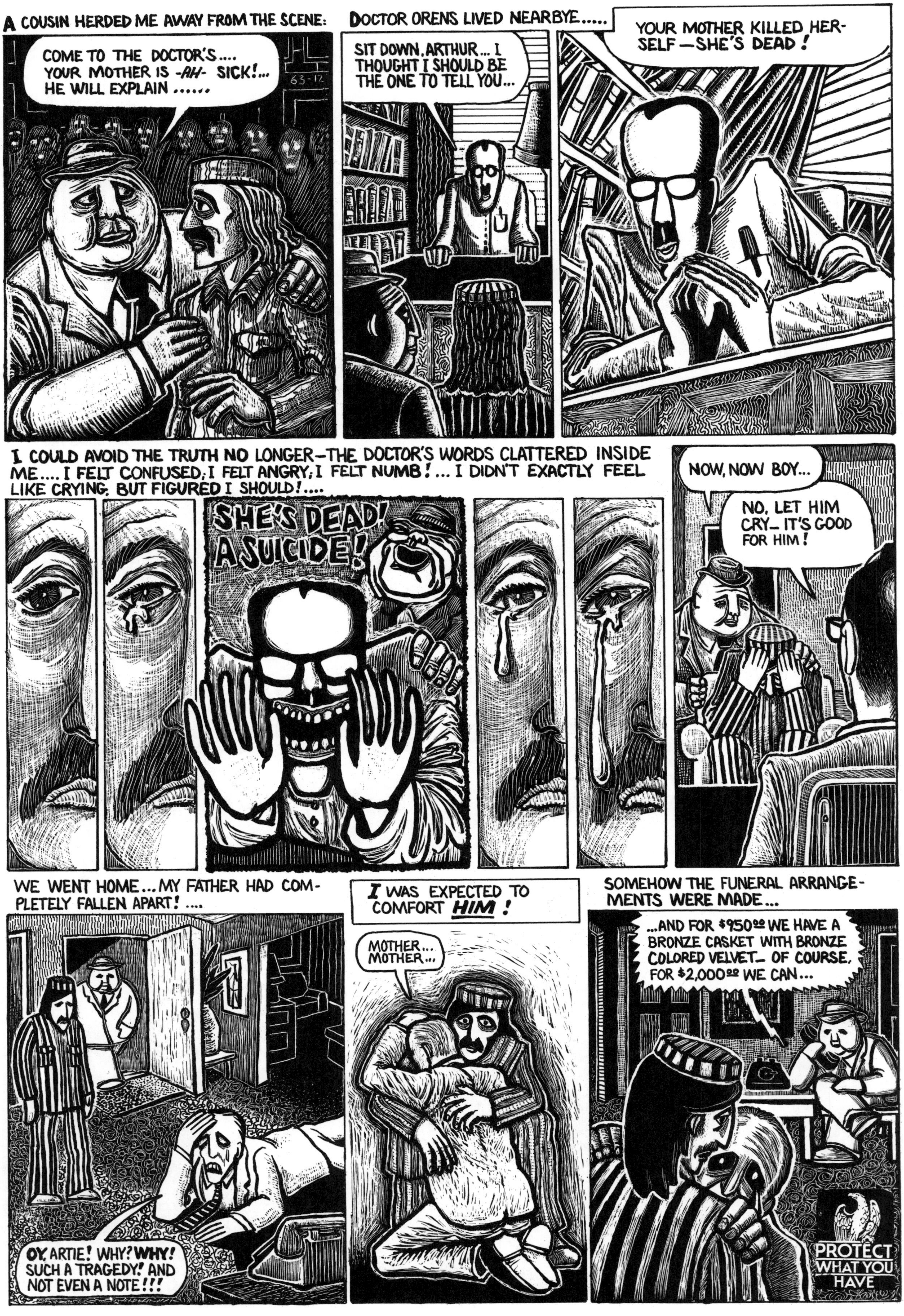
A COUSIN HERDED ME AWAY FROM THE SCENE:
COME TO THE DOCTOR'S.... YOUR MOTHER IS -AH- SICK!... HE WILL EXPLAIN......
63-12
DOCTOR ORENS LIVED NEARBYE.....
SIT DOWN, ARTHUR... I THOUGHT I SHOULD BE THE ONE TO TELL YOU...
YOUR MOTHER KILLED HER-SELF—SHE'S DEAD!
I COULD AVOID THE TRUTH NO LONGER—THE DOCTOR'S WORDS CLATTERED INSIDE ME.... I FELT CONFUSED; I FELT ANGRY; I FELT NUMB!... I DIDN'T EXACTLY FEEL LIKE CRYING, BUT FIGURED I SHOULD!....
SHE'S DEAD! A SUICIDE!
NOW, NOW BOY...
NO, LET HIM CRY— IT'S GOOD FOR HIM!
WE WENT HOME... MY FATHER HAD COM-PLETELY FALLEN APART!....
OY, ARTIE! WHY? WHY! SUCH A TRAGEDY! AND NOT EVEN A NOTE!!!
I WAS EXPECTED TO COMFORT HIM!
MOTHER... MOTHER...
SOMEHOW THE FUNERAL ARRANGE-MENTS WERE MADE...
...AND FOR $950.00 WE HAVE A BRONZE CASKET WITH BRONZE COLORED VELVET— OF COURSE, FOR $2,000.00 WE CAN...
PROTECT WHAT YOU HAVE

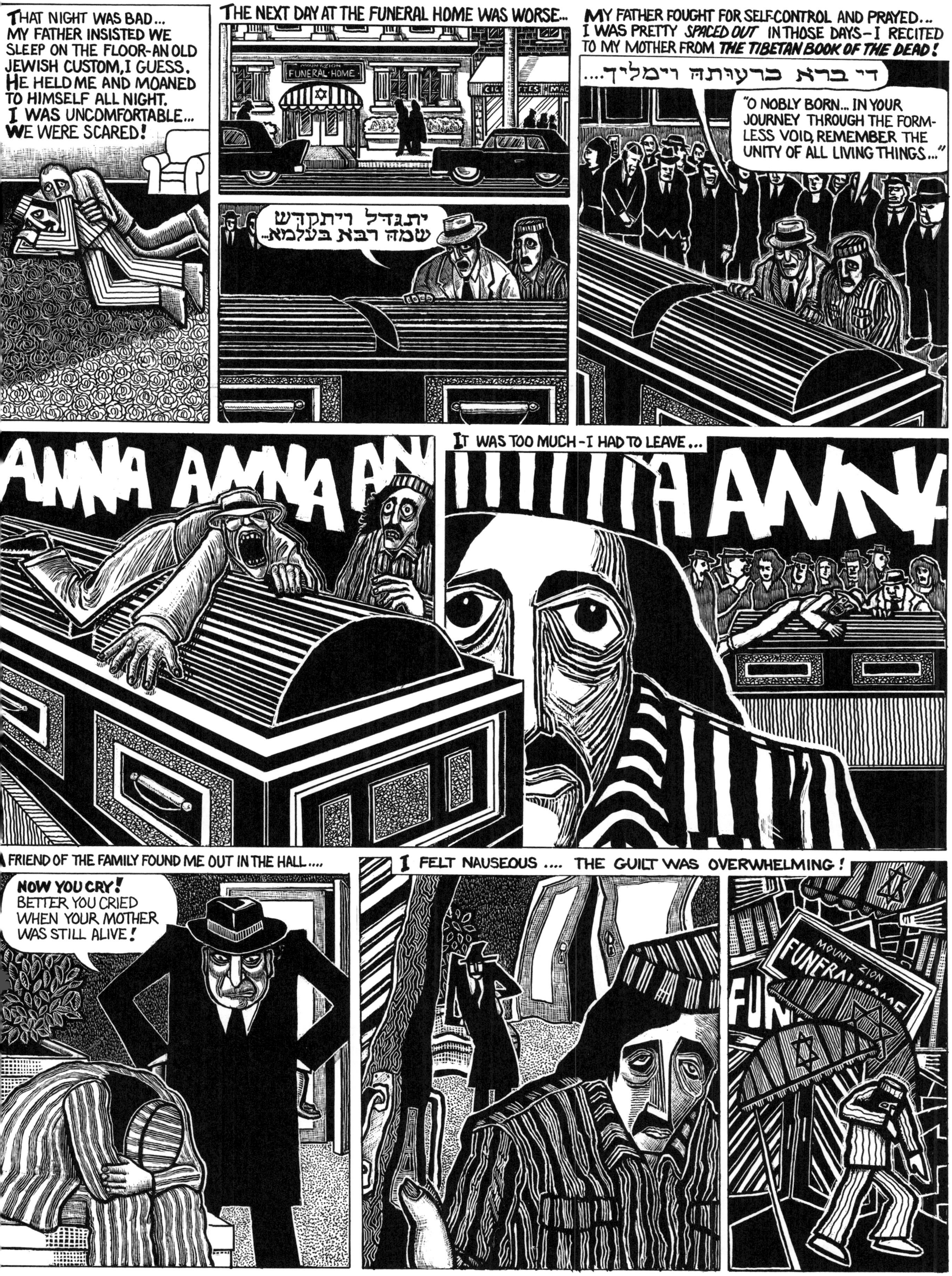
THAT NIGHT WAS BAD... MY FATHER INSISTED WE SLEEP ON THE FLOOR-AN OLD JEWISH CUSTOM, I GUESS. HE HELD ME AND MOANED TO HIMSELF ALL NIGHT. I WAS UNCOMFORTABLE... WE WERE SCARED!
THE NEXT DAY AT THE FUNERAL HOME WAS WORSE...
MOUNT ZION
FUNERAL HOME
יתגדל ויתקדש שמה רבא בעלמא...
MY FATHER FOUGHT FOR SELF-CONTROL AND PRAYED... I WAS PRETTY *SPACED OUT* IN THOSE DAYS- I RECITED TO MY MOTHER FROM ***THE TIBETAN BOOK OF THE DEAD!***
די ברא כרעותה וימליך...
"O NOBLY BORN... IN YOUR JOURNEY THROUGH THE FORMLESS VOID, REMEMBER THE UNITY OF ALL LIVING THINGS..."
ANNA ANNA AN
IT WAS TOO MUCH-I HAD TO LEAVE...
IIIIIIA ANNA
A FRIEND OF THE FAMILY FOUND ME OUT IN THE HALL....
NOW YOU CRY! BETTER YOU CRIED WHEN YOUR MOTHER WAS STILL ALIVE!
I FELT NAUSEOUS .... THE GUILT WAS OVERWHELMING!
MOUNT ZION
FUNERAL HOME
FUN

© art spiegelman, 1972

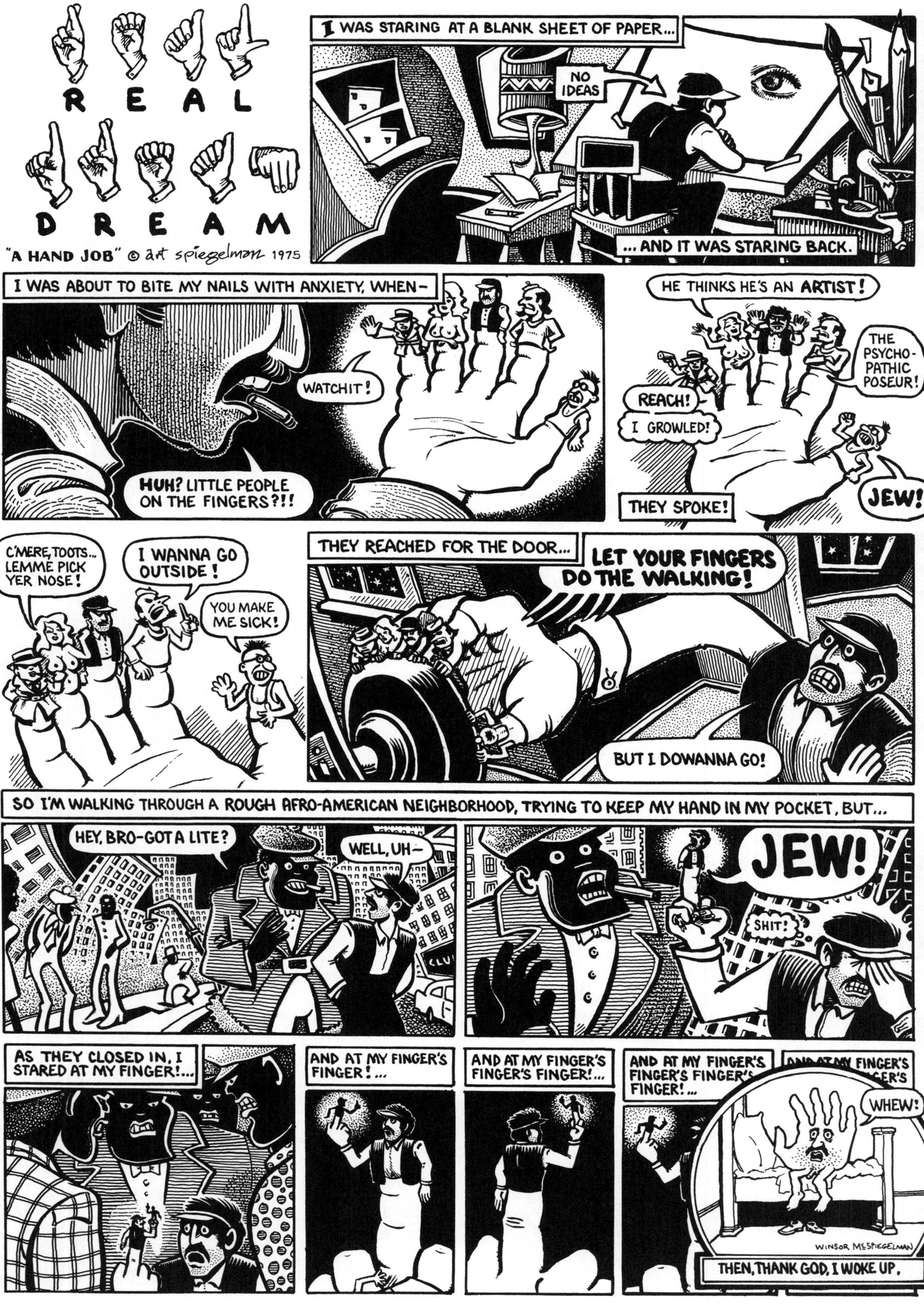
REAL
DREAM
"A HAND JOB" © art spiegelman 1975
I WAS STARING AT A BLANK SHEET OF PAPER...
NO IDEAS
...AND IT WAS STARING BACK.
I WAS ABOUT TO BITE MY NAILS WITH ANXIETY, WHEN—
WATCHIT!
HUH? LITTLE PEOPLE ON THE FINGERS?!!
HE THINKS HE'S AN ARTIST!
THE PSYCHO-PATHIC POSEUR!
REACH!
I GROWLED!
THEY SPOKE!
JEW!
C'MERE, TOOTS... LEMME PICK YER NOSE!
I WANNA GO OUTSIDE!
YOU MAKE ME SICK!
THEY REACHED FOR THE DOOR...
LET YOUR FINGERS DO THE WALKING!
BUT I DOWANNA GO!
SO I'M WALKING THROUGH A ROUGH AFRO-AMERICAN NEIGHBORHOOD, TRYING TO KEEP MY HAND IN MY POCKET, BUT...
HEY, BRO-GOT A LITE?
WELL, UH—
JEW!
SHIT!
AS THEY CLOSED IN, I STARED AT MY FINGER!...
AND AT MY FINGER'S FINGER!...
AND AT MY FINGER'S FINGER'S FINGER!...
AND AT MY FINGER'S FINGER'S FINGER'S FINGER!...
WHEW!
WINSOR McSPIEGELMAN
THEN, THANK GOD, I WOKE UP.

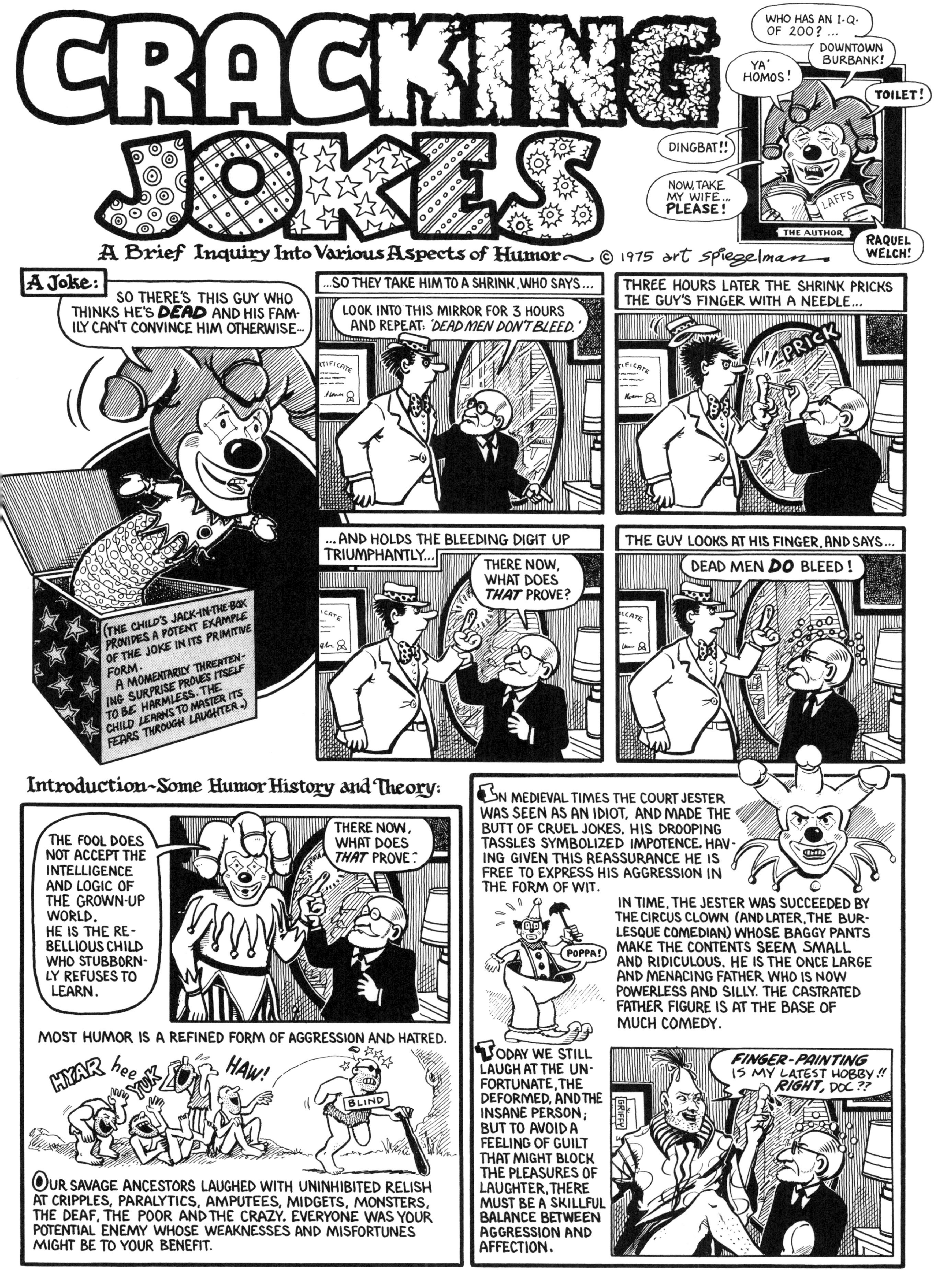
CRACKING JOKES
WHO HAS AN I.Q. OF 200? ...
DOWNTOWN BURBANK!
YA' HOMOS!
TOILET!
DINGBAT!!
NOW, TAKE MY WIFE... PLEASE!
LAFFS
THE AUTHOR
RAQUEL WELCH!
A Brief Inquiry Into Various Aspects of Humor ~ © 1975 art spiegelman
A Joke:
SO THERE'S THIS GUY WHO THINKS HE'S DEAD AND HIS FAMILY CAN'T CONVINCE HIM OTHERWISE...
(THE CHILD'S JACK-IN-THE-BOX PROVIDES A POTENT EXAMPLE OF THE JOKE IN ITS PRIMITIVE FORM. A MOMENTARILY THREATENING SURPRISE PROVES ITSELF TO BE HARMLESS. THE CHILD LEARNS TO MASTER ITS FEARS THROUGH LAUGHTER.)
...SO THEY TAKE HIM TO A SHRINK, WHO SAYS...
LOOK INTO THIS MIRROR FOR 3 HOURS AND REPEAT: 'DEAD MEN DON'T BLEED.'
THREE HOURS LATER THE SHRINK PRICKS THE GUY'S FINGER WITH A NEEDLE...
PRICK
...AND HOLDS THE BLEEDING DIGIT UP TRIUMPHANTLY...
THERE NOW, WHAT DOES THAT PROVE?
THE GUY LOOKS AT HIS FINGER, AND SAYS...
DEAD MEN DO BLEED!
Introduction ~ Some Humor History and Theory:
THE FOOL DOES NOT ACCEPT THE INTELLIGENCE AND LOGIC OF THE GROWN-UP WORLD. HE IS THE REBELLIOUS CHILD WHO STUBBORNLY REFUSES TO LEARN.
THERE NOW, WHAT DOES THAT PROVE?
MOST HUMOR IS A REFINED FORM OF AGGRESSION AND HATRED.
HYAR hee YUK HAW!
BLIND
OUR SAVAGE ANCESTORS LAUGHED WITH UNINHIBITED RELISH AT CRIPPLES, PARALYTICS, AMPUTEES, MIDGETS, MONSTERS, THE DEAF, THE POOR AND THE CRAZY. EVERYONE WAS YOUR POTENTIAL ENEMY WHOSE WEAKNESSES AND MISFORTUNES MIGHT BE TO YOUR BENEFIT.
IN MEDIEVAL TIMES THE COURT JESTER WAS SEEN AS AN IDIOT, AND MADE THE BUTT OF CRUEL JOKES. HIS DROOPING TASSLES SYMBOLIZED IMPOTENCE. HAVING GIVEN THIS REASSURANCE HE IS FREE TO EXPRESS HIS AGGRESSION IN THE FORM OF WIT.
POPPA!
IN TIME, THE JESTER WAS SUCCEEDED BY THE CIRCUS CLOWN (AND LATER, THE BURLESQUE COMEDIAN) WHOSE BAGGY PANTS MAKE THE CONTENTS SEEM SMALL AND RIDICULOUS. HE IS THE ONCE LARGE AND MENACING FATHER WHO IS NOW POWERLESS AND SILLY. THE CASTRATED FATHER FIGURE IS AT THE BASE OF MUCH COMEDY.
TODAY WE STILL LAUGH AT THE UNFORTUNATE, THE DEFORMED, AND THE INSANE PERSON; BUT TO AVOID A FEELING OF GUILT THAT MIGHT BLOCK THE PLEASURES OF LAUGHTER, THERE MUST BE A SKILLFUL BALANCE BETWEEN AGGRESSION AND AFFECTION.
GRIFFY
FINGER-PAINTING IS MY LATEST HOBBY!! RIGHT, DOC??

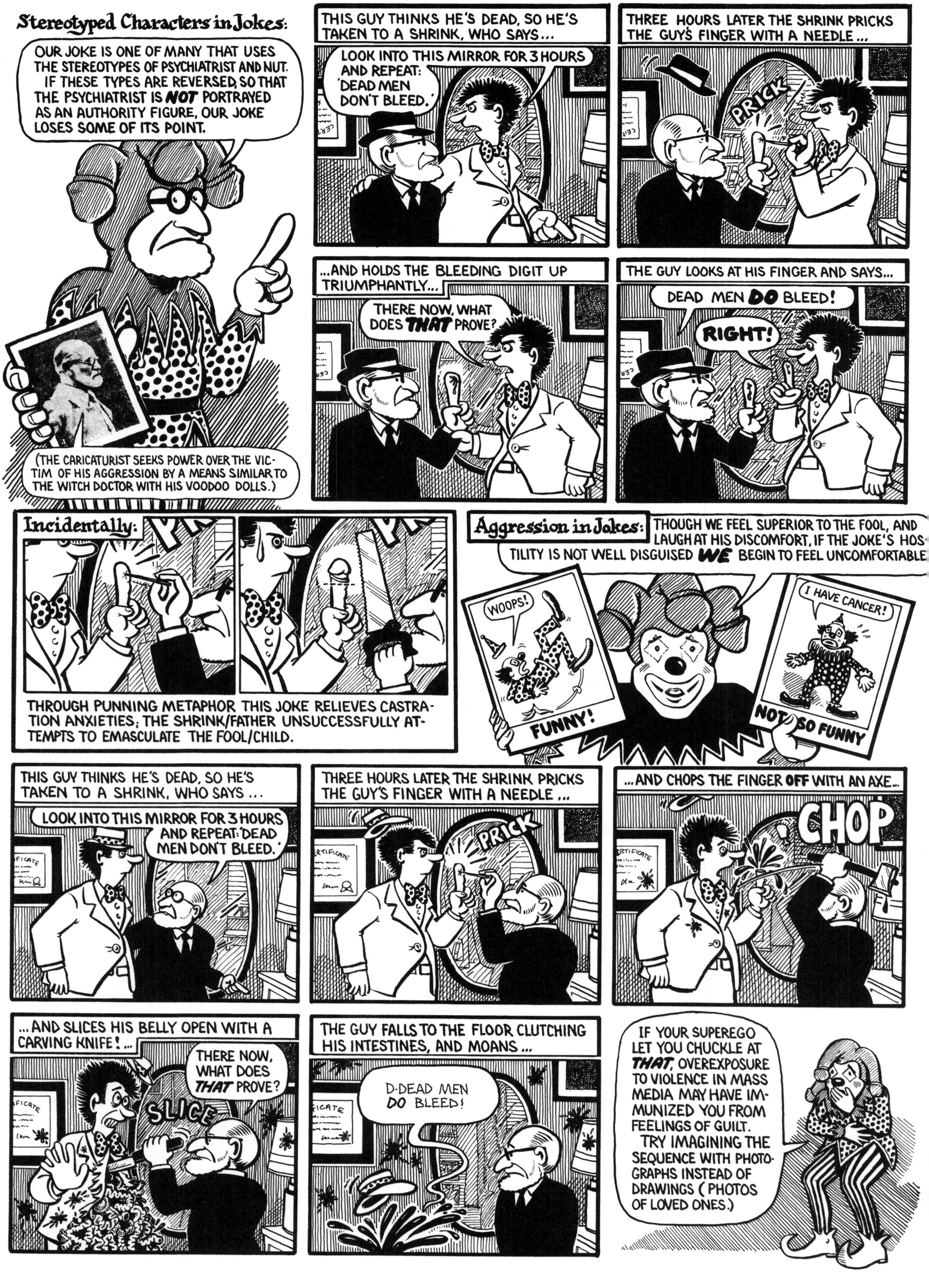

Stereotyped Characters in Jokes:
OUR JOKE IS ONE OF MANY THAT USES THE STEREOTYPES OF PSYCHIATRIST AND NUT. IF THESE TYPES ARE REVERSED, SO THAT THE PSYCHIATRIST IS NOT PORTRAYED AS AN AUTHORITY FIGURE, OUR JOKE LOSES SOME OF ITS POINT.
(THE CARICATURIST SEEKS POWER OVER THE VICTIM OF HIS AGGRESSION BY A MEANS SIMILAR TO THE WITCH DOCTOR WITH HIS VOODOO DOLLS.)
THIS GUY THINKS HE'S DEAD, SO HE'S TAKEN TO A SHRINK, WHO SAYS...
LOOK INTO THIS MIRROR FOR 3 HOURS AND REPEAT: 'DEAD MEN DON'T BLEED.'
THREE HOURS LATER THE SHRINK PRICKS THE GUY'S FINGER WITH A NEEDLE...
PRICK
...AND HOLDS THE BLEEDING DIGIT UP TRIUMPHANTLY...
THERE NOW, WHAT DOES THAT PROVE?
THE GUY LOOKS AT HIS FINGER AND SAYS...
DEAD MEN DO BLEED!
RIGHT!
Incidentally:
THROUGH PUNNING METAPHOR THIS JOKE RELIEVES CASTRATION ANXIETIES; THE SHRINK/FATHER UNSUCCESSFULLY ATTEMPTS TO EMASCULATE THE FOOL/CHILD.
Aggression in Jokes:
THOUGH WE FEEL SUPERIOR TO THE FOOL, AND LAUGH AT HIS DISCOMFORT, IF THE JOKE'S HOSTILITY IS NOT WELL DISGUISED WE BEGIN TO FEEL UNCOMFORTABLE
WOOPS!
FUNNY!
I HAVE CANCER!
NOT SO FUNNY
THIS GUY THINKS HE'S DEAD, SO HE'S TAKEN TO A SHRINK, WHO SAYS...
LOOK INTO THIS MIRROR FOR 3 HOURS AND REPEAT: 'DEAD MEN DON'T BLEED.'
THREE HOURS LATER THE SHRINK PRICKS THE GUY'S FINGER WITH A NEEDLE...
PRICK
...AND CHOPS THE FINGER OFF WITH AN AXE...
CHOP
...AND SLICES HIS BELLY OPEN WITH A CARVING KNIFE!...
THERE NOW, WHAT DOES THAT PROVE?
SLICE
THE GUY FALLS TO THE FLOOR CLUTCHING HIS INTESTINES, AND MOANS...
D-DEAD MEN DO BLEED!
IF YOUR SUPEREGO LET YOU CHUCKLE AT THAT, OVEREXPOSURE TO VIOLENCE IN MASS MEDIA MAY HAVE IMMUNIZED YOU FROM FEELINGS OF GUILT.
TRY IMAGINING THE SEQUENCE WITH PHOTOGRAPHS INSTEAD OF DRAWINGS (PHOTOS OF LOVED ONES.)

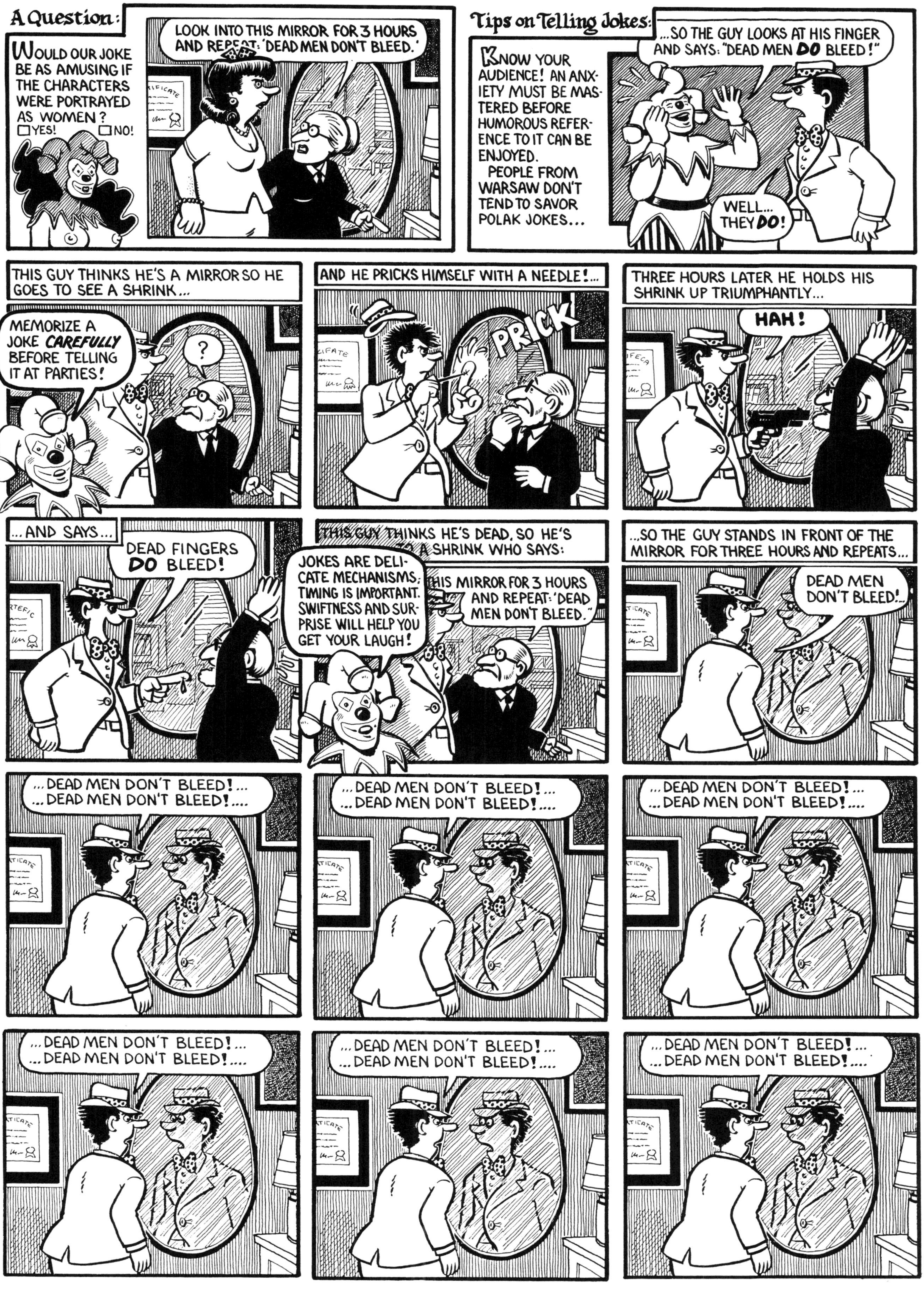
A Question:
WOULD OUR JOKE BE AS AMUSING IF THE CHARACTERS WERE PORTRAYED AS WOMEN?
☐ YES! ☐ NO!
LOOK INTO THIS MIRROR FOR 3 HOURS AND REPEAT: 'DEAD MEN DON'T BLEED.'
Tips on Telling Jokes:
KNOW YOUR AUDIENCE! AN ANXIETY MUST BE MASTERED BEFORE HUMOROUS REFERENCE TO IT CAN BE ENJOYED.
PEOPLE FROM WARSAW DON'T TEND TO SAVOR POLAK JOKES...
...SO THE GUY LOOKS AT HIS FINGER AND SAYS: "DEAD MEN DO BLEED!"
WELL... THEY DO!
THIS GUY THINKS HE'S A MIRROR SO HE GOES TO SEE A SHRINK...
MEMORIZE A JOKE CAREFULLY BEFORE TELLING IT AT PARTIES!
?
AND HE PRICKS HIMSELF WITH A NEEDLE!...
PRICK
THREE HOURS LATER HE HOLDS HIS SHRINK UP TRIUMPHANTLY...
HAH!
...AND SAYS...
DEAD FINGERS DO BLEED!
THIS GUY THINKS HE'S DEAD, SO HE'S
A SHRINK WHO SAYS:
JOKES ARE DELICATE MECHANISMS; TIMING IS IMPORTANT. SWIFTNESS AND SURPRISE WILL HELP YOU GET YOUR LAUGH!
THIS MIRROR FOR 3 HOURS AND REPEAT: 'DEAD MEN DON'T BLEED.'
...SO THE GUY STANDS IN FRONT OF THE MIRROR FOR THREE HOURS AND REPEATS...
DEAD MEN DON'T BLEED!...
...DEAD MEN DON'T BLEED!... ...DEAD MEN DON'T BLEED!....
...DEAD MEN DON'T BLEED!... ...DEAD MEN DON'T BLEED!....
...DEAD MEN DON'T BLEED!... ...DEAD MEN DON'T BLEED!....
...DEAD MEN DON'T BLEED!... ...DEAD MEN DON'T BLEED!....
...DEAD MEN DON'T BLEED!... ...DEAD MEN DON'T BLEED!....
...DEAD MEN DON'T BLEED!... ...DEAD MEN DON'T BLEED!....

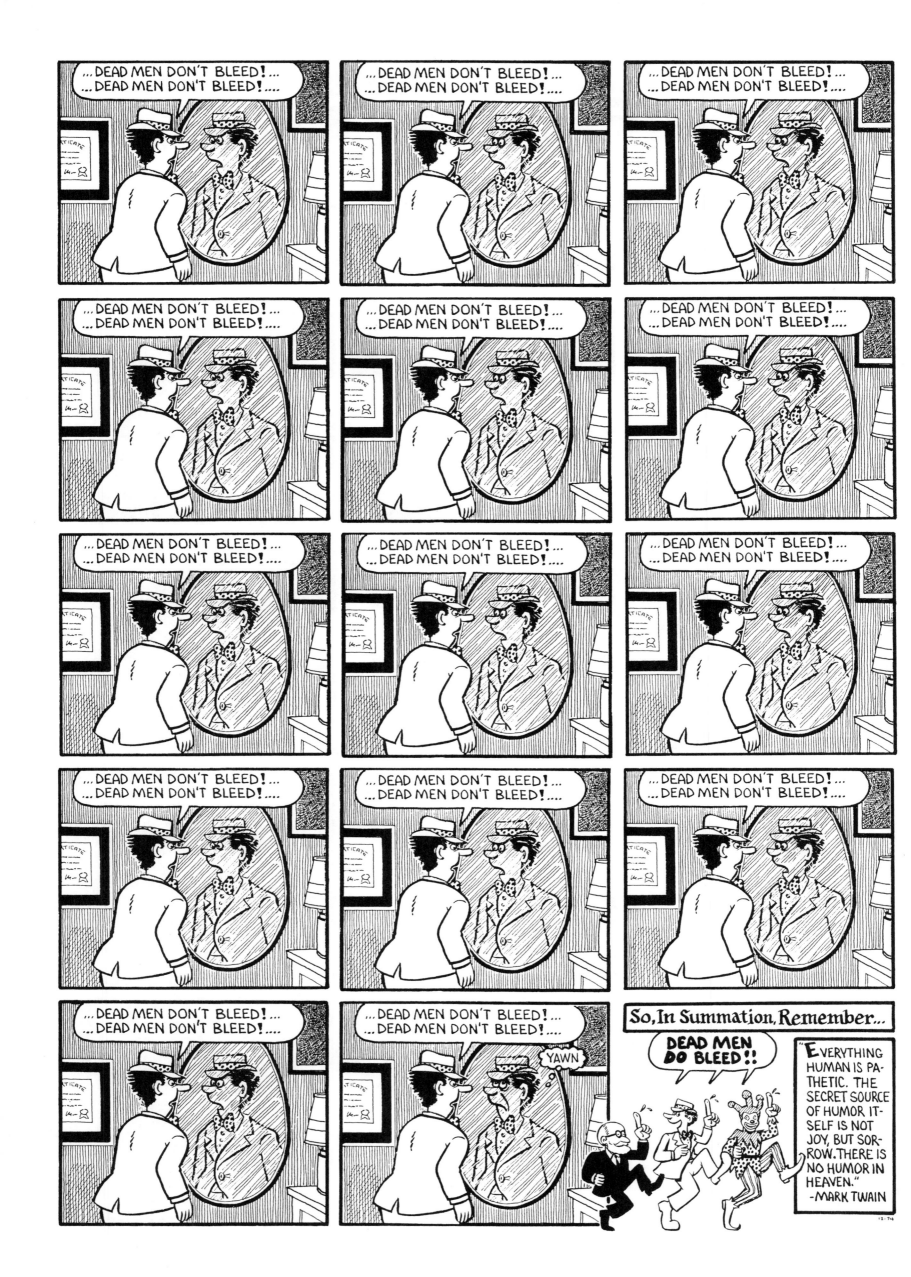

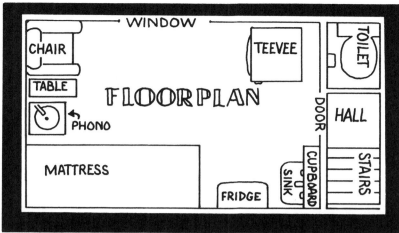

FLOORPLAN

WINDOW / CHAIR / TABLE / PHONO / MATTRESS / TEEVEE / TOILET / DOOR / HALL / CUPBOARD / SINK / STAIRS / FRIDGE

DON'T GET AROUND MUCH ANYMORE

TO BE READ TO THE ACCOMPANIMENT OF A DRIPPING FAUCET, SLOWLY.

copyright © 1973 ~ art spiegelman

MY CABLE BILL IS PAID UP FOR THE NEXT THREE MONTHS ....

...I HAVE A ROOM WITH A VIEW....

...AND WHOEVER LIVED HERE BEFORE LEFT A STACK OF LIFE MAGAZINES.

THE SOUND DOESN'T WORK ON THE TEEVEE...

...BUT I DON'T CARE. I OWN A RECORD!

THE REFRIGERATOR IS EMPTY.

THERE ARE SOME CRACKERS IN THE CUPBOARD, AND ...

...ALL THE WATER I CAN USE POURS OUT OF THE FAUCET WITH A FLICK OF THE WRIST.

...I DON'T GET AROUND MUCH ANYMORE...

THE CRACKERS AND WATER SHOULD KEEP ME GOING.

SEE THAT KID OUTSIDE?...

HE'S BEEN BOUNCING THAT BALL FOR HOURS ...YOU'D THINK HE'D GET TIRED!

I READ IN LIFE THAT ANN MARGRET IS MAKING A COMEBACK...

AT LAST A STAR? — SHE STILL HAS DOUBTS! / put more flavor in your life

AT LAST A STAR?— SHE STILL HAS DOUBTS! / put more flavor in your life

...AND MELVIN MADDOCKS DIDN'T CARE FOR HERMAN WOUK'S NEW BOOK!

THE RECORD SKIPS. IT HAS A SCRATCH.

-DID I TELL YOU THE REFRIGERATOR IS EMPTY?

3-12-73

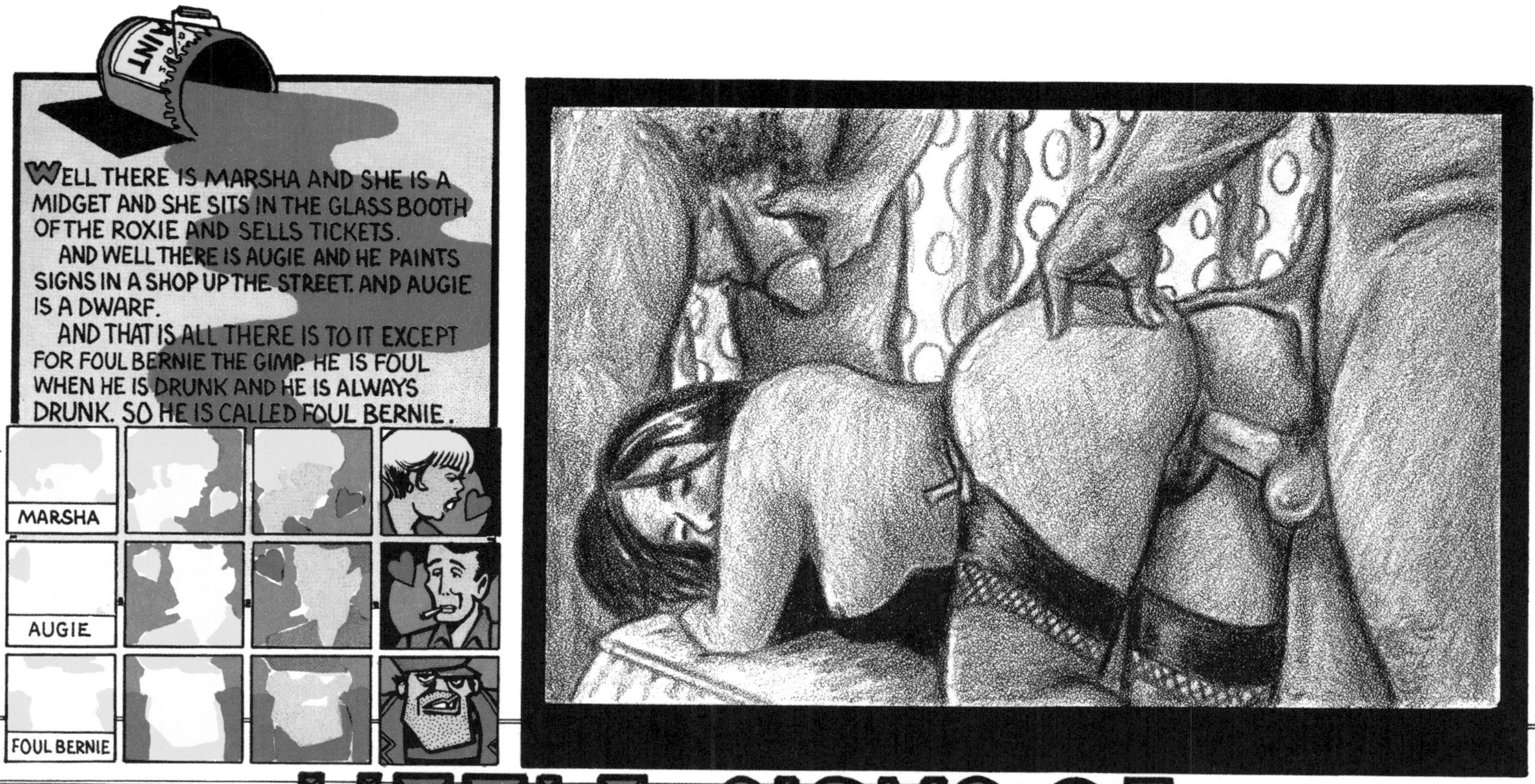
PAINT
WELL THERE IS MARSHA AND SHE IS A MIDGET AND SHE SITS IN THE GLASS BOOTH OF THE ROXIE AND SELLS TICKETS.
AND WELL THERE IS AUGIE AND HE PAINTS SIGNS IN A SHOP UP THE STREET. AND AUGIE IS A DWARF.
AND THAT IS ALL THERE IS TO IT EXCEPT FOR FOUL BERNIE THE GIMP. HE IS FOUL WHEN HE IS DRUNK AND HE IS ALWAYS DRUNK. SO HE IS CALLED FOUL BERNIE.
MARSHA
AUGIE
FOUL BERNIE

LITTLE SIGNS OF PASSION

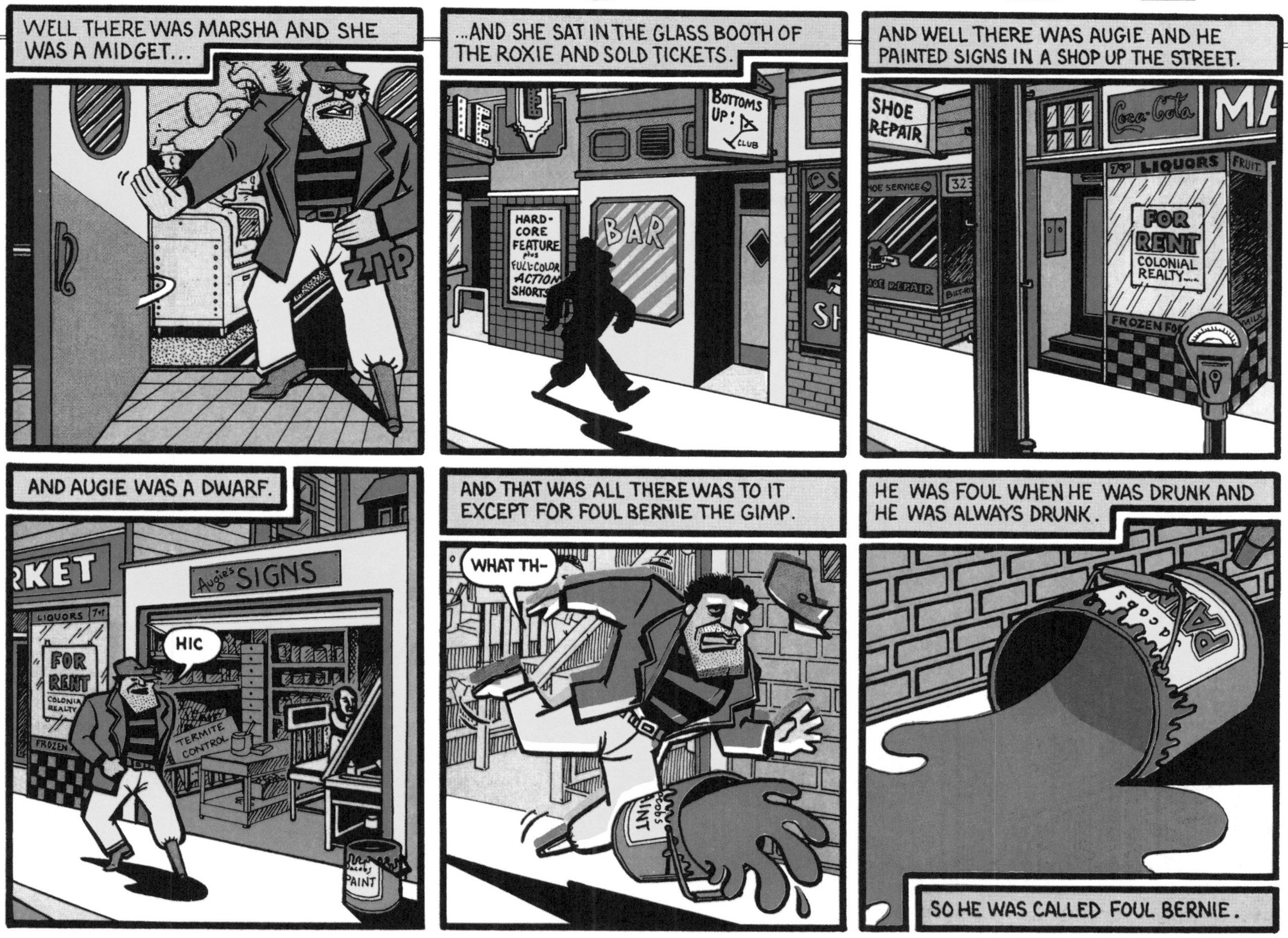
WELL THERE WAS MARSHA AND SHE WAS A MIDGET...
ZIP
...AND SHE SAT IN THE GLASS BOOTH OF THE ROXIE AND SOLD TICKETS.
BOTTOMS UP! CLUB
HARD-CORE FEATURE plus FULL-COLOR ACTION SHORTS
BAR
AND WELL THERE WAS AUGIE AND HE PAINTED SIGNS IN A SHOP UP THE STREET.
SHOE REPAIR
Coca-Cola
LIQUORS
FOR RENT COLONIAL REALTY
AND AUGIE WAS A DWARF.
Augie's SIGNS
HIC
FOR RENT
TERMITE CONTROL
PAINT
AND THAT WAS ALL THERE WAS TO IT EXCEPT FOR FOUL BERNIE THE GIMP.
WHAT TH-
HE WAS FOUL WHEN HE WAS DRUNK AND HE WAS ALWAYS DRUNK.
SO HE WAS CALLED FOUL BERNIE.

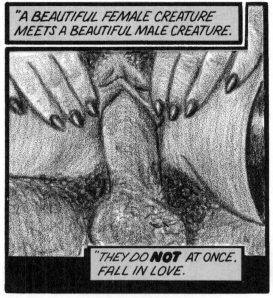

"A BEAUTIFUL FEMALE CREATURE MEETS A BEAUTIFUL MALE CREATURE.

"THEY DO **NOT** AT ONCE, FALL IN LOVE.

"BUT IT IS OBVIOUS TO THE READER FROM THE BEGINNING THAT THEY **OUGHT** TO FALL IN LOVE."

WELL THERE WAS MARSHA AND SHE WAS A MIDGET.

"BECAUSE READERS ARE LIKE THAT THEY WILL BE OVERJOYED AND FOR SOME PATHOLOGICAL REASON DOWNRIGHT SURPRISED WHEN...

"AFTER CARRYING YOUR STORY THROUGH THE OPENING PAGES YOU DO HAVE THE BEAUTIFUL MALE AND FEMALE CREATURES FALL IN LOVE."

AND WELL THERE WAS AUGIE AND HE PAINTED SIGNS IN A SHOP UP THE STREET.

"KNOW WHAT SADISM IS?"

HIC
HYAR!
HYAR!

AND SHE SAT IN THE GLASS BOOTH OF THE ROXIE AND SOLD TICKETS.

"WELL IF YOU DON'T, DON'T BE EMBARRASSED.

WANNA HEAR SOMETHIN' FUNNY?... I WALKED PAST SOME BROAD YESTERDAY. IT WAS REAL WINDY!

"NOBODY ELSE KNOWS FOR SURE EITHER."

"IT IS A STRANGE LATENCY IN THE HUMAN MIND,...

"STRONG IN SOME, WEAK IN OTHERS,...

"WHICH MAKES THE AVERAGE READER BECOME RESTLESS IF THE **C**OURSE OF **T**RUE **L**OVE RUNS SMOOTHLY."

...SO DE WIND BLOWS HER SKOIT UP OVER HER WAIST AND SHE AIN'T GOT NO **UNDERPANTS** ON!...

AND AUGIE WAS A DWARF.

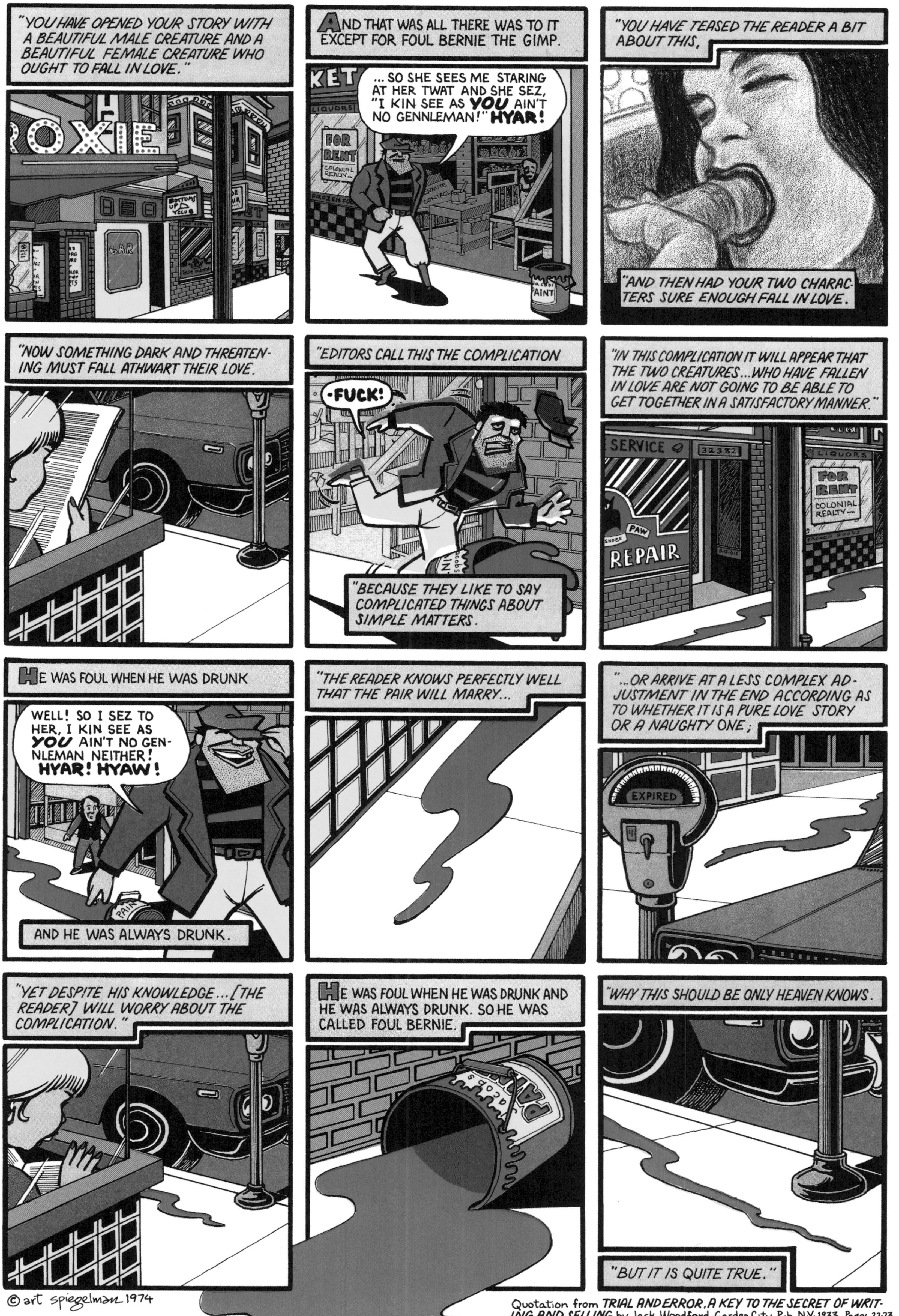
"YOU HAVE OPENED YOUR STORY WITH A BEAUTIFUL MALE CREATURE AND A BEAUTIFUL FEMALE CREATURE WHO OUGHT TO FALL IN LOVE."
ROXIE
BAR
AND THAT WAS ALL THERE WAS TO IT EXCEPT FOR FOUL BERNIE THE GIMP.
... SO SHE SEES ME STARING AT HER TWAT AND SHE SEZ, "I KIN SEE AS YOU AIN'T NO GENNLEMAN!" HYAR!
LIQUORS
FOR RENT
COLONIAL REALTY
PAINT
"YOU HAVE TEASED THE READER A BIT ABOUT THIS,
"AND THEN HAD YOUR TWO CHARACTERS SURE ENOUGH FALL IN LOVE.
"NOW SOMETHING DARK AND THREATENING MUST FALL ATHWART THEIR LOVE.
"EDITORS CALL THIS THE COMPLICATION
•FUCK!
"BECAUSE THEY LIKE TO SAY COMPLICATED THINGS ABOUT SIMPLE MATTERS.
"IN THIS COMPLICATION IT WILL APPEAR THAT THE TWO CREATURES... WHO HAVE FALLEN IN LOVE ARE NOT GOING TO BE ABLE TO GET TOGETHER IN A SATISFACTORY MANNER."
SERVICE
32382
LIQUORS
FOR RENT
COLONIAL REALTY
PAW
SHOES
REPAIR
HE WAS FOUL WHEN HE WAS DRUNK
WELL! SO I SEZ TO HER, I KIN SEE AS YOU AIN'T NO GENNLEMAN NEITHER! HYAR! HYAW!
AND HE WAS ALWAYS DRUNK.
"THE READER KNOWS PERFECTLY WELL THAT THE PAIR WILL MARRY...
"...OR ARRIVE AT A LESS COMPLEX ADJUSTMENT IN THE END ACCORDING AS TO WHETHER IT IS A PURE LOVE STORY OR A NAUGHTY ONE;
EXPIRED
"YET DESPITE HIS KNOWLEDGE ... [THE READER] WILL WORRY ABOUT THE COMPLICATION."
HE WAS FOUL WHEN HE WAS DRUNK AND HE WAS ALWAYS DRUNK. SO HE WAS CALLED FOUL BERNIE.
Jacobs PAINT
"WHY THIS SHOULD BE ONLY HEAVEN KNOWS.
"BUT IT IS QUITE TRUE."

Quotation from *TRIAL AND ERROR, A KEY TO THE SECRET OF WRITING AND SELLING* by Jack Woodford; Garden City Pub. N.Y. 1933. Pages 22-23.

"ONLY THE DEAD KNOW BROOKLYN."
-THOMAS WOLFE

New ork Journal
© art spiegelman 1975

WEATHER: HOT, HUMID, VERY NOISY.

AIR: UNACCEPTABLE

SPIEGELMAN MOVES TO N.Y. "FEELS DEPRESSED!!!"

US/RUSS LINK UP OUTER SPACE

Complete story inside

FINDS APARTMENT

GETS LIBRARY CARD

6/3. Rented an apartment in Brooklyn—Kitchen is in a closet with a sink the size of an ashtray. I hear that the girl who lived here before jumped in front of a subway.

TRACING FORM

MY SUPER

The apartment faces the once posh Saint George — now a welfare hotel. There was a murder there this week; the third in 4 years.

6/7. Went to the Museum of Modern Art. Saw enlarged photos of cigarette butts...Didn't meet any women.

Took the subway home. Squashed 17 roaches, got tired and went to sleep.

6/8. Called my father (he lives in Queens) but didn't want him to know I'm in town; I'm not ready to cope with him yet...

YES DAD, THE WEATHER IN SAN FRANCISCO *IS* BEAUTIFUL...YES...NO, I MEAN YES...YES...YES...

CRIMESTOPPER'S TEXTBOOK: TOWEL OVER RECEIVER MUFFLES SOUND INTO *"LONG DISTANCE."*

6/11. Had to go to some meeting. Afterwards some of us went to Billy's — a nondescript topless bar on 6th avenue near 23rd street...

Juke Box

The dancer squatted down on the table in front of the drunks. They ate her out, then put rolled up dollar bills in her cunt...

?

She came over and asked me for a dollar. I *handed* it to her...

WHAT'S TH' MATTER, HONEY, IT WON'T BITE!

...I'd never been panhandled that way before.

Took the subway home. Felt depressed. Squashed 11 roaches before going to sleep.

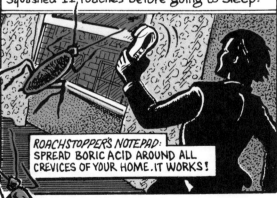

ROACHSTOPPER'S NOTEPAD: SPREAD BORIC ACID AROUND ALL CREVICES OF YOUR HOME. IT WORKS!

6/16 Went to a ritzy party for business reasons. Didn't know anyone. Tried to be polite.

...BORIC ACID REALLY WORKS! Y'KNOW, SAN FRANCISCO DOESN'T HAVE ROACHES!

THERE'S A *LOT* SAN FRANCISCO DOESN'T HAVE!

SNEER!

We...ome and read Before the Deluge, a b..k about Berlin before World War II.

6...int George hotel is twelve stories h... I spent most of today thinking about going to the roof and jumping off...

...Maybe...i... to start seeing a shrink. I..skeptical, but most of my friends in New York go regularly.

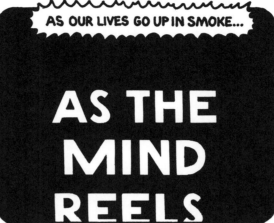

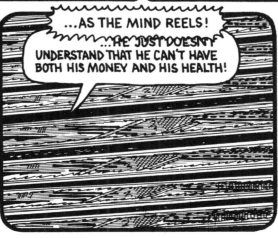

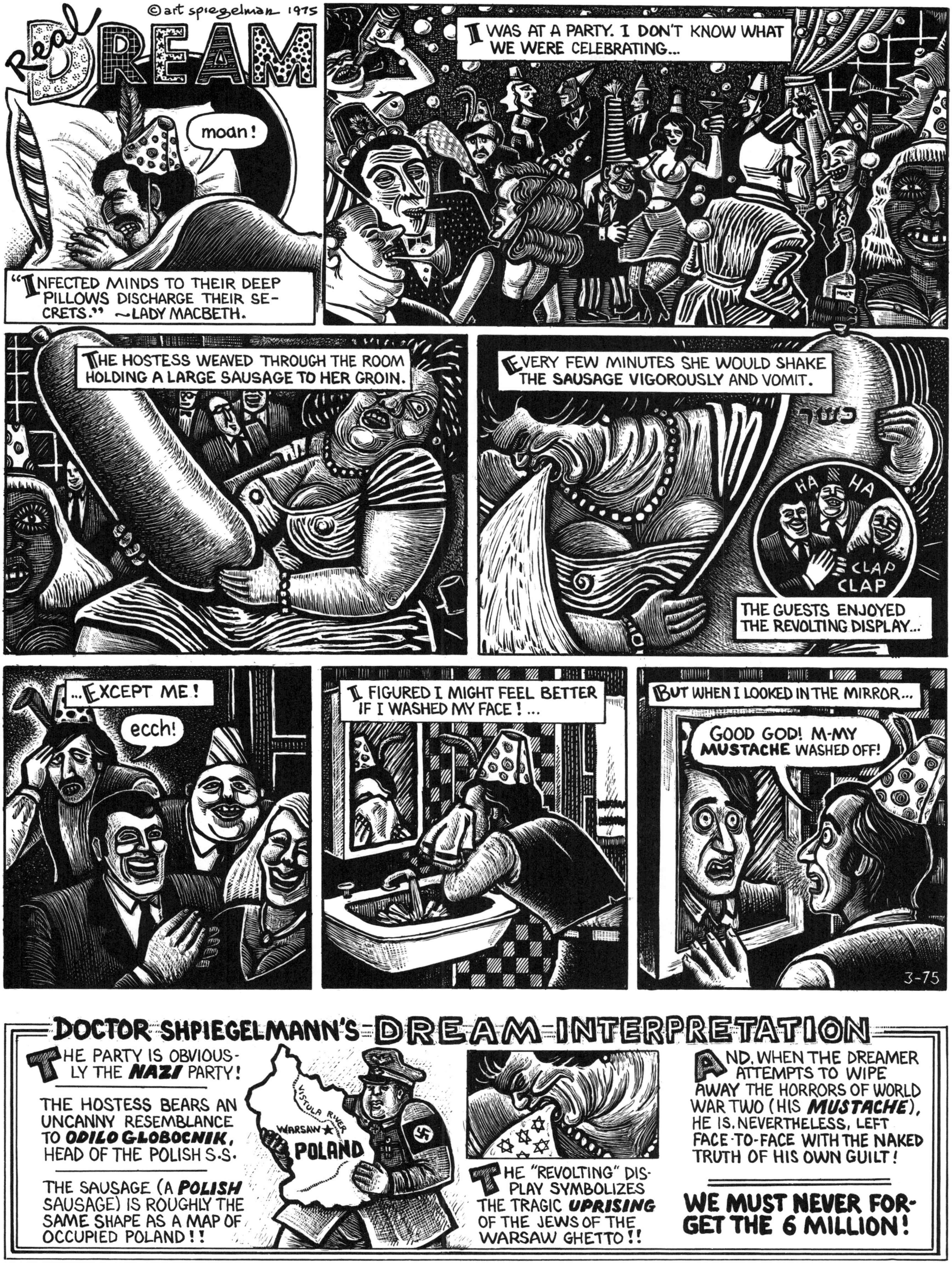
©art spiegelman 1975
Real DREAM
moan!
"INFECTED MINDS TO THEIR DEEP PILLOWS DISCHARGE THEIR SECRETS." ~LADY MACBETH.
I WAS AT A PARTY. I DON'T KNOW WHAT WE WERE CELEBRATING...
THE HOSTESS WEAVED THROUGH THE ROOM HOLDING A LARGE SAUSAGE TO HER GROIN.
EVERY FEW MINUTES SHE WOULD SHAKE THE SAUSAGE VIGOROUSLY AND VOMIT.
כשר
HA HA
CLAP CLAP
THE GUESTS ENJOYED THE REVOLTING DISPLAY...
...EXCEPT ME!
ecch!
I FIGURED I MIGHT FEEL BETTER IF I WASHED MY FACE! ...
BUT WHEN I LOOKED IN THE MIRROR...
GOOD GOD! M-MY MUSTACHE WASHED OFF!
3-75
DOCTOR SHPIEGELMANN'S DREAM INTERPRETATION
THE PARTY IS OBVIOUSLY THE NAZI PARTY!
THE HOSTESS BEARS AN UNCANNY RESEMBLANCE TO ODILO GLOBOCNIK, HEAD OF THE POLISH S.S.
THE SAUSAGE (A POLISH SAUSAGE) IS ROUGHLY THE SAME SHAPE AS A MAP OF OCCUPIED POLAND!!
VISTULA RIVER
WARSAW
POLAND
THE "REVOLTING" DISPLAY SYMBOLIZES THE TRAGIC UPRISING OF THE JEWS OF THE WARSAW GHETTO!!
AND, WHEN THE DREAMER ATTEMPTS TO WIPE AWAY THE HORRORS OF WORLD WAR TWO (HIS MUSTACHE), HE IS, NEVERTHELESS, LEFT FACE-TO-FACE WITH THE NAKED TRUTH OF HIS OWN GUILT!
WE MUST NEVER FORGET THE 6 MILLION!

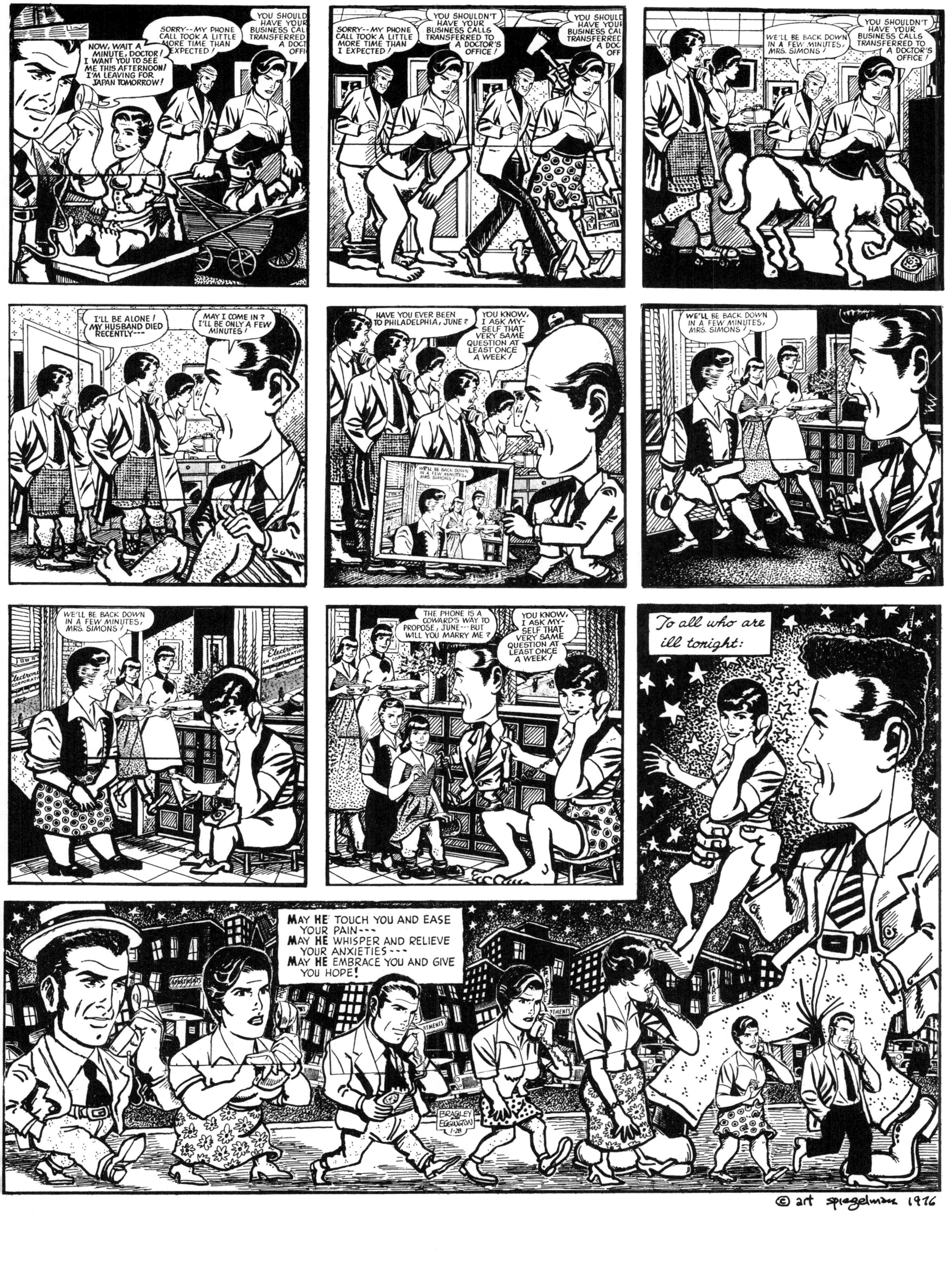
NOW, WAIT A MINUTE, DOCTOR! I WANT YOU TO SEE ME THIS AFTERNOON! I'M LEAVING FOR JAPAN TOMORROW!
SORRY--MY PHONE CALL TOOK A LITTLE MORE TIME THAN I EXPECTED!
YOU SHOULD HAVE YOUR BUSINESS CALL TRANSFERRED A DOCT OFFI
SORRY--MY PHONE CALL TOOK A LITTLE MORE TIME THAN I EXPECTED!
YOU SHOULDN'T HAVE YOUR BUSINESS CALLS TRANSFERRED TO A DOCTOR'S OFFICE!
YOU SHOULD HAVE YOUR BUSINESS CAL TRANSFERRED A DOC OFF
WE'LL BE BACK DOWN IN A FEW MINUTES, MRS. SIMONS!
YOU SHOULDN'T HAVE YOUR BUSINESS CALLS TRANSFERRED TO A DOCTOR'S OFFICE!
I'LL BE ALONE! MY HUSBAND DIED RECENTLY---
MAY I COME IN? I'LL BE ONLY A FEW MINUTES!
HAVE YOU EVER BEEN TO PHILADELPHIA, JUNE?
YOU KNOW, I ASK MY-SELF THAT VERY SAME QUESTION AT LEAST ONCE A WEEK!
WE'LL BE BACK DOWN IN A FEW MINUTES, MRS. SIMONS!
WE'LL BE BACK DOWN IN A FEW MINUTES, MRS. SIMONS!
WE'LL BE BACK DOWN IN A FEW MINUTES, MRS. SIMONS!
THE PHONE IS A COWARD'S WAY TO PROPOSE, JUNE---BUT WILL YOU MARRY ME?
YOU KNOW, I ASK MY-SELF THAT VERY SAME QUESTION AT LEAST ONCE A WEEK!
To all who are ill tonight:
MAY HE TOUCH YOU AND EASE YOUR PAIN---
MAY HE WHISPER AND RELIEVE YOUR ANXIETIES---
MAY HE EMBRACE YOU AND GIVE YOU HOPE!
BRADLEY EGGINGTON 1-28

"AS THEY STARTED OUT THE DOOR, GERTRUDE HANDED PICASSO...THE COMICS SECTION FROM ONE OF THE AMERICAN SUNDAY PAPERS: THE PAINTER WAS AN AVID FOLLOWER OF THE KATZENJAMMER KIDS AND OF LITTLE JIMMY. PICASSO BEAMED AND THANKED HER."

Chapter One: THE SHORT GOODBYE!
ACE HOLE
MIDGET DETECTI
ACE HOLE
GRETA
POTATO-HEAD
I DIDN'T REALLY WANT THE JOB - BUT I NEEDED THE DOUGH... 25 DUCATS POST HASTE OR THEY'D REPOSSESS MY HAT-AND WITHOUT IT WHAT WOULD I USE FOR AN OFFICE ?!!
©art spiegelman 1974
IT WAS A MEAN AND VICIOUS CAPER IN A MEAN AND VICIOUS CITY... LAURENCE POTATO-HEAD, THE ART DEALER, HIRED ME ...
...I WAS TO DIG UP ONE AL FLOOGLEMAN, A BIRD WHO'D PASSED HIM SOME BUM PICASSOS!
I DIDN'T WANT THE JOB, BUT... DOWN THESE MEAN STREETS A MIDGET MUST GO!
IT WAS TOUGH SCARING UP A LINE ON FLOOGLEMAN... I LEARNED HE'D BEEN A SMALL-CHANGE UNDERGROUND CARTOONIST!
WHEN TOUGH PORNO LAWS PUT HIM OUT OF BUSINESS, I GUESS HE STEPPED UP INTO THE FORGERY RACKET!
?
...A GOOD LOOKING FRAIL CRUISED PAST ME.... CALL IT A HUNCH, BUT I DECIDED TO TAIL HER!
SHIT!...
...I'M BEING SHADOWED!
MY OPTICS CHEERFULLY CRUISED HER FANCY CURVES DOWN THE BLOCK. SHE WHEELED THE CORNER BEFORE I DID...
AIEEEEEKKK!
BANG!
A SHOT AND A SCREAM! MY BLOOD FROZE INTO POPSICLES!... I TURNED THE CORNER FAST, LIKE SOME CLOWN TURNING THE PAGES OF A GOOD FUNNY-BOOK!
ZOOM

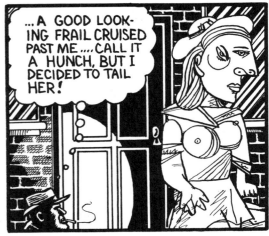

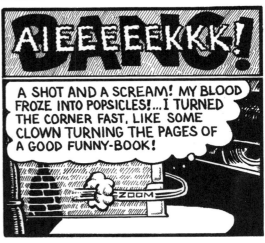

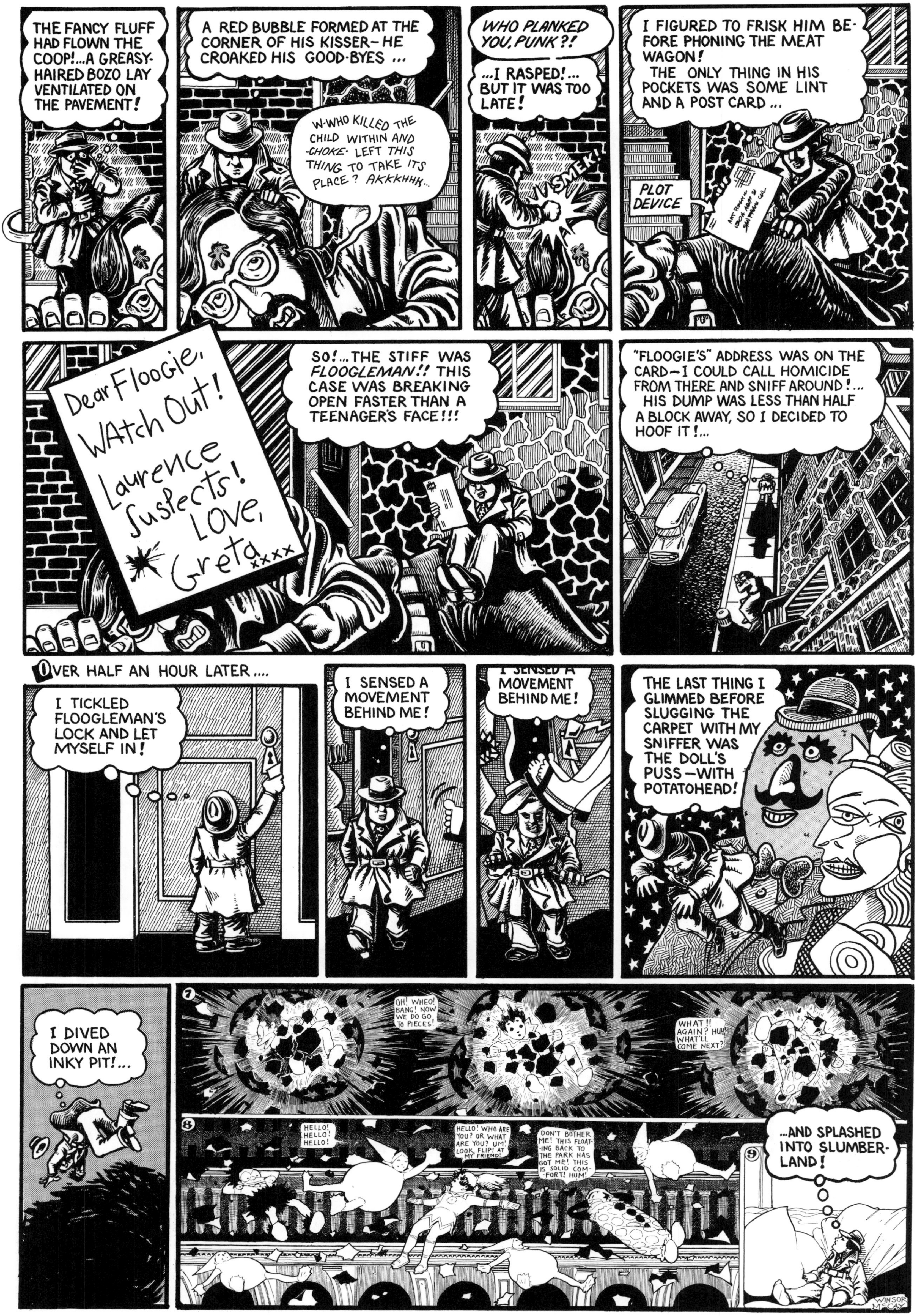
THE FANCY FLUFF HAD FLOWN THE COOP!...A GREASY-HAIRED BOZO LAY VENTILATED ON THE PAVEMENT!
A RED BUBBLE FORMED AT THE CORNER OF HIS KISSER—HE CROAKED HIS GOOD-BYES ...
W-WHO KILLED THE CHILD WITHIN AND -CHOKE- LEFT THIS THING TO TAKE ITS PLACE? AKKKHHH...
WHO PLANKED YOU, PUNK?!
...I RASPED!... BUT IT WAS TOO LATE!
SMEK!
I FIGURED TO FRISK HIM BEFORE PHONING THE MEAT WAGON!
THE ONLY THING IN HIS POCKETS WAS SOME LINT AND A POST CARD...
PLOT DEVICE
Dear Floogie, WAtch Out! Laurence Suspects! LOVE, Greta xxxx
SO!...THE STIFF WAS FLOOGLEMAN!! THIS CASE WAS BREAKING OPEN FASTER THAN A TEENAGER'S FACE!!!
"FLOOGIE'S" ADDRESS WAS ON THE CARD—I COULD CALL HOMICIDE FROM THERE AND SNIFF AROUND!...
HIS DUMP WAS LESS THAN HALF A BLOCK AWAY, SO I DECIDED TO HOOF IT!...
OVER HALF AN HOUR LATER....
I TICKLED FLOOGLEMAN'S LOCK AND LET MYSELF IN!
I SENSED A MOVEMENT BEHIND ME!
I SENSED A MOVEMENT BEHIND ME!
THE LAST THING I GLIMMED BEFORE SLUGGING THE CARPET WITH MY SNIFFER WAS THE DOLL'S PUSS—WITH POTATOHEAD!
I DIVED DOWN AN INKY PIT!...
7
OH! WHEO! BANG! NOW WE DO GO TO PIECES!
WHAT!! AGAIN? HUH! WHAT'LL COME NEXT?
8
HELLO! HELLO! HELLO!
HELLO! WHO ARE YOU? OR WHAT ARE YOU? UM! LOOK, FLIP! AT MY FRIEND!
DON'T BOTHER ME! THIS FLOATING BACK TO THE PARK HAS GOT ME! THIS IS SOLID COMFORT! HUM!
9
...AND SPLASHED INTO SLUMBERLAND!
WINSOR McCAY

Chapter Two: NO POCKETS IN A MIDGET, DON'T THEY?

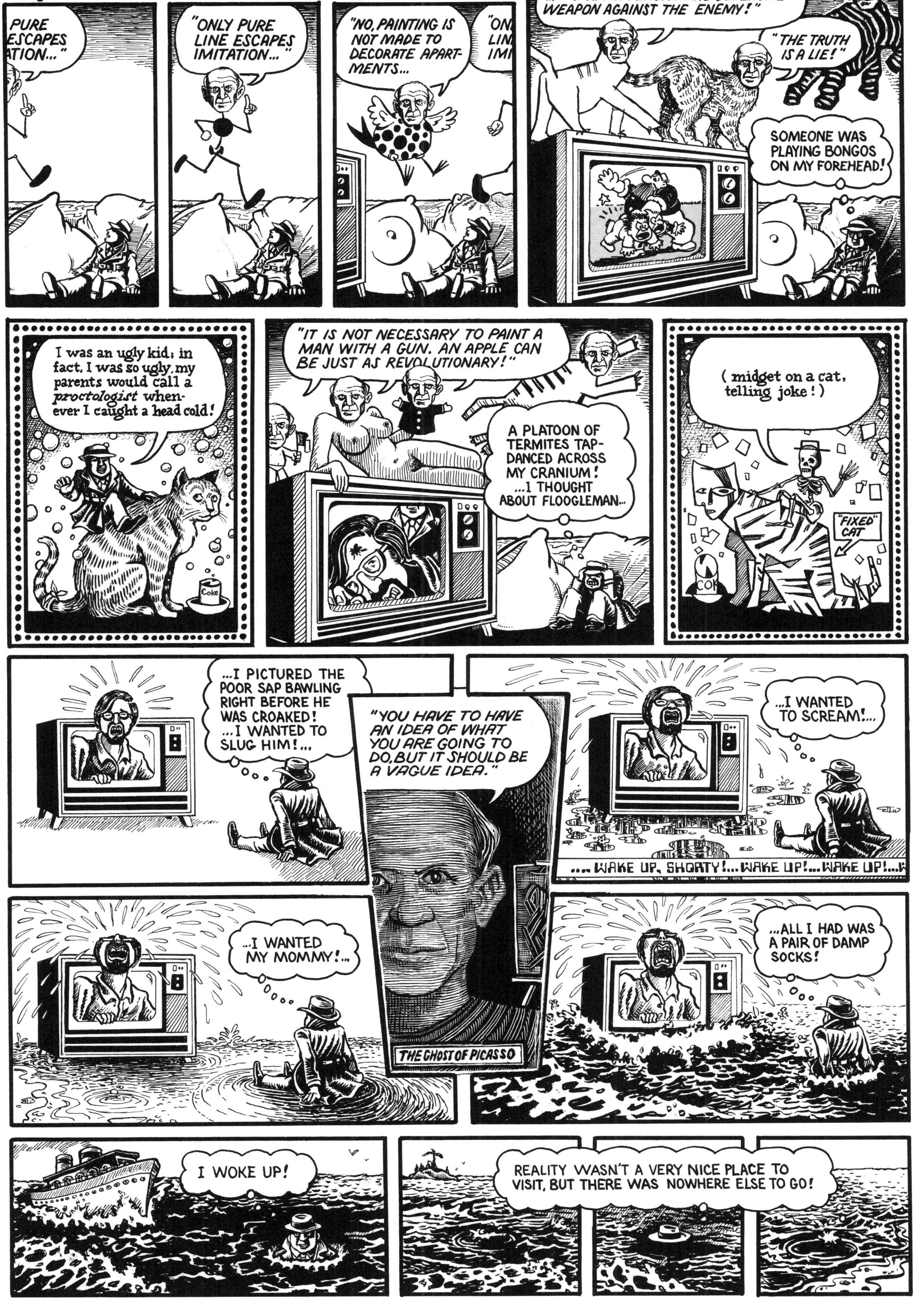

PURE
ESCAPES
ATION..."
"ONLY PURE LINE ESCAPES IMITATION..."
"NO, PAINTING IS NOT MADE TO DECORATE APART-MENTS...
"ON
LIN
IMI
...IT'S AN OFFENSIVE AND DEFENSIVE WEAPON AGAINST THE ENEMY!"
"THE TRUTH IS A LIE!"
SOMEONE WAS PLAYING BONGOS ON MY FOREHEAD!
I was an ugly kid; in fact, I was so ugly, my parents would call a *proctologist* whenever I caught a head cold!
Coke
"IT IS NOT NECESSARY TO PAINT A MAN WITH A GUN. AN APPLE CAN BE JUST AS REVOLUTIONARY!"
A PLATOON OF TERMITES TAP-DANCED ACROSS MY CRANIUM! ...I THOUGHT ABOUT FLOOGLEMAN...
(midget on a cat, telling joke!)
"FIXED" CAT
COK
...I PICTURED THE POOR SAP BAWLING RIGHT BEFORE HE WAS CROAKED! ...I WANTED TO SLUG HIM!...
"YOU HAVE TO HAVE AN IDEA OF WHAT YOU ARE GOING TO DO, BUT IT SHOULD BE A VAGUE IDEA."
THE GHOST OF PICASSO
...I WANTED TO SCREAM!...
....WAKE UP, SHORTY!...WAKE UP!...WAKE UP!...W
...I WANTED MY MOMMY!...
...ALL I HAD WAS A PAIR OF DAMP SOCKS!
I WOKE UP!
REALITY WASN'T A VERY NICE PLACE TO VISIT, BUT THERE WAS NOWHERE ELSE TO GO!

"WE ARTISTS ARE INDESTRUCTABLE...."

"...EVEN IN A PRISON OR IN A CONCENTRATION CAMP, I WOULD BE ALMIGHTY IN MY OWN WORLD OF ART...."

"...EVEN IF I HAD TO PAINT MY PICTURES WITH MY WET TONGUE ON THE DUSTY FLOOR OF MY CELL."

REALITY WASN'T A VERY NICE PLACE TO VISIT....

HURRY ACE WAKE UP

...I WOKE UP - MY GRAY MATTER FELT LIKE SHATTERED SILLY PUTTY!

IF THIS KIND OF TREATMENT KEPT UP, I **WOULD** NEED A PROCTOLOGIST FOR MY HEADACHES!

THE SCENERY HAD CHANGED WHILE I SNOOZED. I WAS IN POTATOHEAD'S APARTMENT AND HIS MOLL WAS STROKING MY BROW... THINGS WERE LOOKING UP A LITTLE!

We Must Hurry!!!...

My Husband Went out for some tobacco. He Left me here to keep an Eye on you!

THIS DAME...

He'll Kill You! **Kill You!!** But... I... don't... want you... Dead!

...WAS DYNAMITE! SHE HAD MORE SIDES THAN A REVOLVING DOOR!

HER KISSES MADE MY TOENAILS QUIVER, BUT BUSINESS HAD TO COME BEFORE I COULD...

GET ME MY GUN!

I GROWLED!

SHE HANDED IT OVER. I DIDN'T KNOW MUCH ABOUT ART, BUT THIS BABE WAS JAKE WITH ME! I GRINNED AND SAID...

FILL IN THE **DE-TAILS** TOOTSIE.... I DON'T GET THE PICTURE!

Well... Laurence and FlooGleman Were partners....

FlooGleman forged the Paintings; Laurence was the fence...

NOW [B]E WAS [... A]ND SAID...

FILL IN [T]HE **DE-TAILS** [T]OOTSIE [I] DON'T

All went well until I fell for Floogie...

Laurence found out. He went crazy and **m-murdered** him!...

[...TH]E[... TOOTSI]E [I] DON'T GET THE PICTURE!

He tried to set you up as the fall guy, but you knew too much!

"IT FIT LIKE A GLOVE!..."

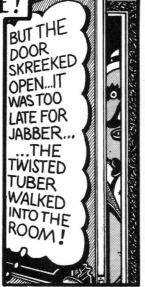

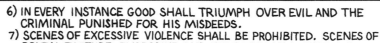

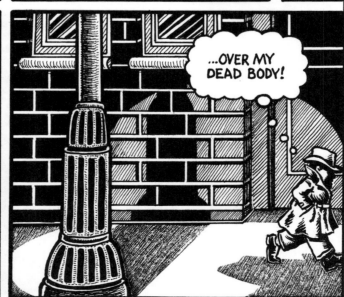

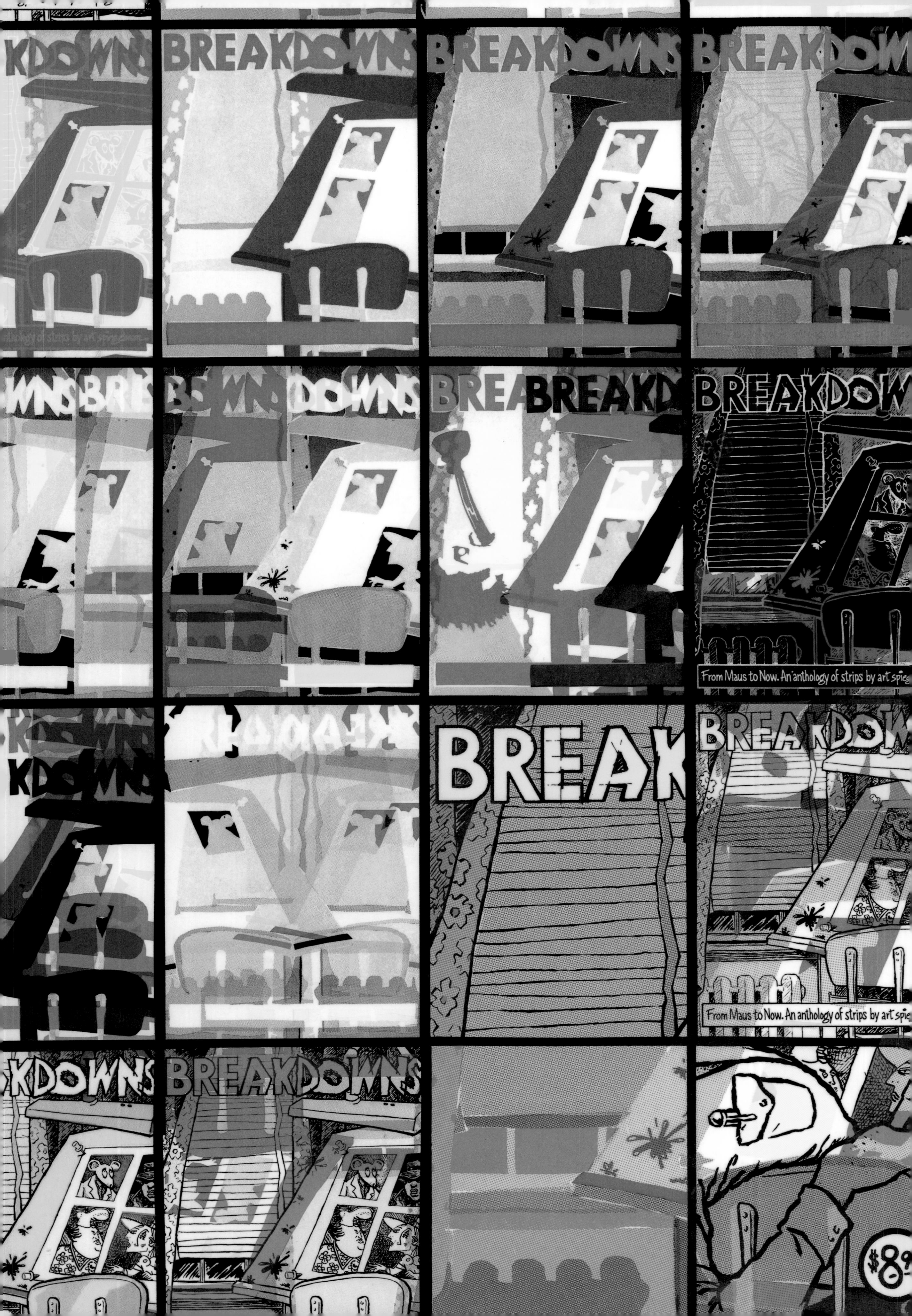

KDOWNS
BREAKDOWNS
From Maus to Now. An anthology of strips by art spieg
BREAK
From Maus to Now. An anthology of strips by art spieg
KDOWNS
BREAKDOWNS

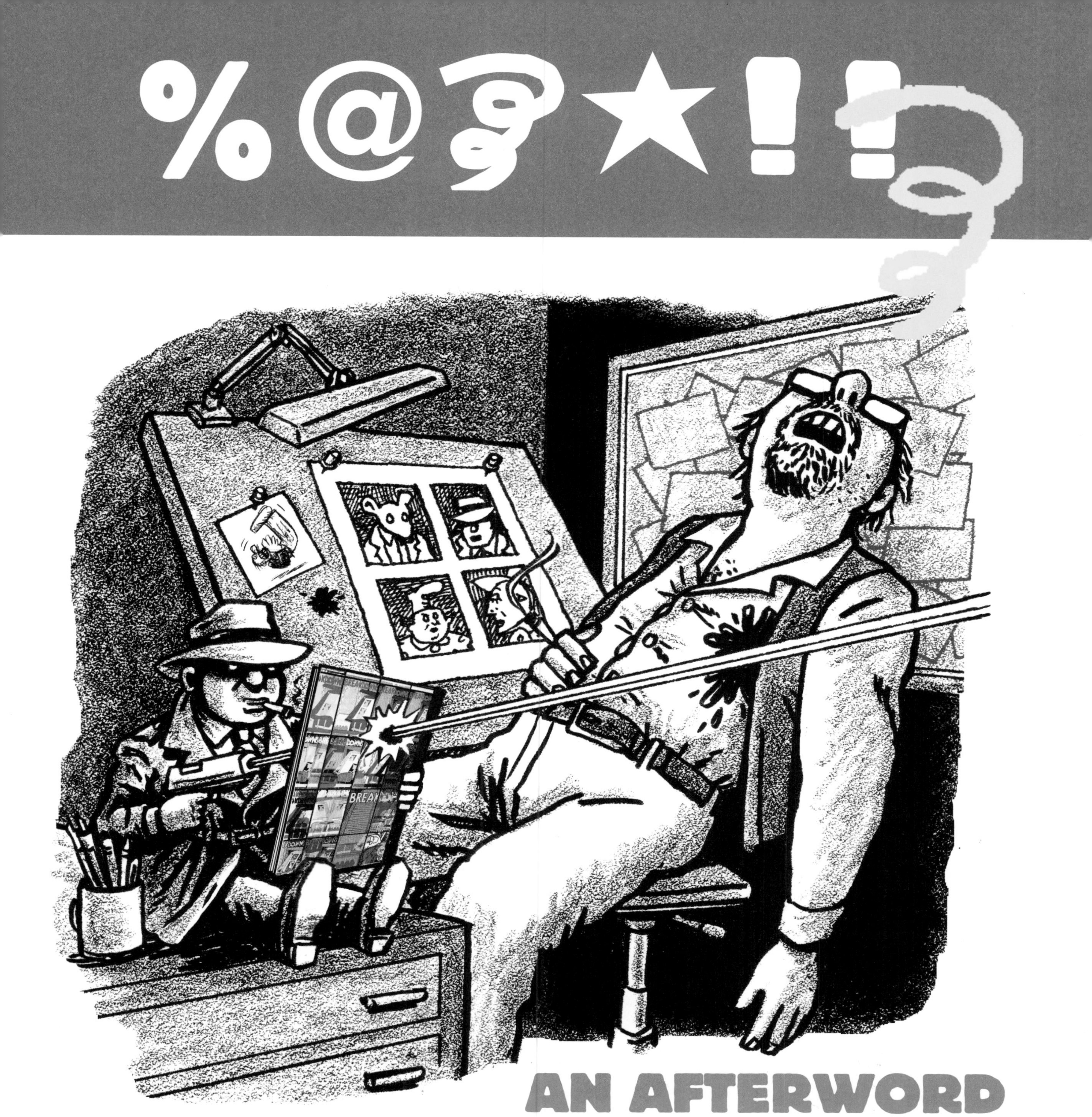

AN AFTERWORD

I envy the wild-eyed, ink-swilling young artist who made the strips gathered in *Breakdowns* thirty years ago. Looking through the work in this skinny book now, it's hard to reconstruct the context—or, maybe, lack of context—in which he first explored the possibilities he saw in the medium he loved. I admire his ambition, his enthusiasm, his single-mindedness and his skinniness. He was on fire, alienated and ignored, but arrogantly certain that his book would be a central artifact in the history of Modernism. Disinterest on the part of most readers and other cartoonists only convinced him he was onto something new in the world. In an underground comix scene that prided itself on breaking taboos, he was breaking the one taboo left standing: he dared to call himself an artist and call his medium an art form.

While the hard-won pages the self-important squirt gathered in *Breakdowns* were among the first maps that led to comics being welcomed into today's bookstores, libraries, museums and universities, he wasn't making a conscious bid for cultural respectability. Once underground cartoonists had unleashed their checkered demons in the cheerfully vernacular medium of comics, he was able to focus on the *grammar* of that vernacular and nail his own personal demons. High Art and Low. Words and Pictures. Form and Content. It all might sound dry and academic, but—*Hell!*—for me then it was a matter of Life and Death.

Breakdowns was published in 1978, against all odds. There was no demand for a deluxe large-format album that collected the scattered handful of short autobiographical and structurally "experimental" comics I'd made between 1972 and 1977—except by me. I had finally found my voice as a cartoonist, and needed to see my strips in a setting separate from the underground comix they had been born in, to understand what I had articulated.

Breakdowns' now confusing subtitle, "From Maus to Now," referred to a 3-page strip that I had done in 1972, not the three hundred-page book in two volumes that grew from that seed years later. The "Now" in the subtitle of course refers to "Then," as it always does once it's uttered; just like

WELL ... WHO'S GOT A GAG FOR ME TODAY ?
art spiegelman 14

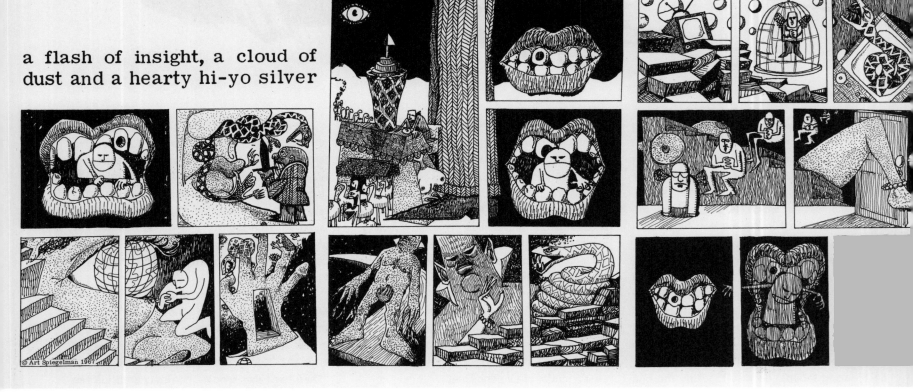

comics, a parade of past moments always presenting a present that is past. The 3-page Maus strip I did back then is the earliest piece included in *Breakdowns*. It followed a stumbling apprenticeship that started before I could read.

In the claustrophobic confines of my immigrant parents' home, comics were my picture window onto American culture. The first fresh air from the outside world came from Carl Barks' *Donald Duck,* John Stanley's *Little Lulu,* and, most penetratingly, from the strong blast of Harvey Kurtzman's *MAD*. As soon as I found out that cartoons weren't exactly natural phenomena—like trees—but were actually made by people, I desperately wanted to be one of the people who made them. The only thing that changed over the years was the kind of cartoons I wanted to make.

I had my first drawing published in 1961, when I was thirteen. I had taken a sheaf of cartoons to a small weekly newspaper in Queens, looking for a gig. Instead, they ran a small feature about me, accompanied by my drawing of Frankenstein, under the humiliating headline: "Budding Artist Wants Attention!" I got a better reception a few years later, when I was a student at the High School of Art and Design—a vocational school for commercial art in midtown Manhattan—and the same paper hired me as a regular freelancer. In high school I started making strange, surreal, and decidedly uncommercial comics between homework assignments. In 1965, I took some of these to the just-launched *East Village Other,* one of the first of the underground weekly papers that helped define what we now call the Sixties. The comics in their first few issues really sucked, so I was sure my work would fit right in. The editor, Walter Bowart, looked my pages over with sympathy if not comprehension, and asked if I could do some strips about sex and drugs. I knew little about either, so I enrolled at Harpur College in Binghamton, NY, and set out to find out about both while dodging the draft.

By 1967, my virginity and mind were both long gone, and I began a hazy period of bouncing from Binghamton to the East Village, San Francisco and back, with pit stops at a psychedelicized commune in Vermont. I drew leaflets printed in runs of a hundred or so, passing them out on street corners and in parks when I wasn't passing out myself. Sometimes in comics format, sometimes in imitation of Fillmore concert posters, they extolled LSD, protested the war and, as often as not, had no discernable message at all.

That year—before Underground Comix were quite definable as such—I first met R. Crumb, visiting him in his Haight-Ashbury apartment as a fellow protégé of Woody Gelman. (Woody was my mentor back in New York, giving me a summer job as an idea man at Topps Chewing Gum, Inc. as soon as I turned eighteen, a position that ended up lasting twenty years and helped subsidize my "career" as an underground cartoonist.) Crumb showed me the unpublished pages he'd recently made, the results of his LSD experiences. To put it as I did then: they totally, like, blew my mind. The work served up a parodic reinvention of lost lowbrow cartoon art styles, rubbery, hairy and convoluted, at a moment when cartoon art was still striving toward the streamlined and minimalist. These pages seemed to be dredged directly from the subconscious, but couldn't glibly be labeled surreal. They were all-too-real, urgent, existential, scary and hilarious, though often without anything as conventional as a punch line.

My own experiments with mind-altering drugs at the time had more banally shifted my ambitions toward becoming At One With the Universe and Achieving Egoless Buddha-hood; the ambition to make Strange Comics that had gripped me in high school came in second. Seeing Crumb's radically

ABOVE: Self-portrait, *The Apex Treasury of Underground Comics,* 1974

BELOW: "A Flash of Insight..." drawn in 1965 or 1966, and described by revered *MAD* artist Wally Wood as "that 3-page *thing* about masturbation" before he published it in the second issue of his proto-underground comic magazine, *Witzend,* in 1967

FACING PAGE. TOP LEFT: Leaflet, 1967
TOP RIGHT: Leaflet, 1967. Reprinted in various underground newspapers and in *Witzend,* #3, 1967

BOTTOM LEFT: Cover, *The East Village Other,* Volume 4, No. 18, 1969
BOTTOM RIGHT: Cover, *The East Village Other,* Volume 4, No. 44, 1969

a flash of insight, a cloud of dust and a hearty hi-yo silver
© Art Spiegelman 1967

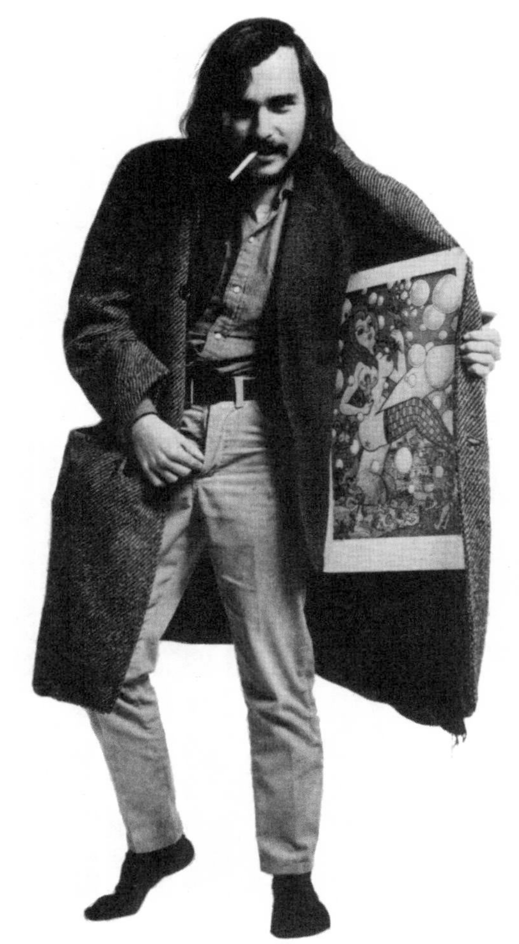

new work in 1967 was a relief. I could leave this comics stuff in his uniquely capable hands and pursue Enlightenment unencumbered, since it would take several lifetimes—reincarnation was then part of my mixed-up mix!—to get anywhere near his achievements. I remember babbling to him about my incipient ideas of what comics might do ("Panels can be inset into bigger panels to show different points in space simultaneously! Repeating panels can freeze the flow of time! Time is an illusion that can be shattered in comics! Showing the same scene from different angles freezes it in time by turning the page into a diagram—an orthographic projection!") and wandering off to nearby Golden Gate Park to drop acid.

As I crash-landed back on Earth over the next couple of years, I tried to absorb what Crumb and other underground cartoonists I admired were up to by badly imitating them all. It made for some very embarrassing work: substandard stabs at erotica and transgressive humor, as well as grotesque exercises in taboo breaking that featured patricide, necrophilia and other misguided eruptions of violence on paper. One of these strips "climaxed" with a character of mine, The Viper, fucking a young boy's severed head in the neck. I wanted to draw the most disturbing images I could think up, and they at least disturbed Crumb's then wife, Dana, enough to bar me from ever visiting her home. I was an enterprising junior member of an exhilarating scene but, man, was I lost.

Several significant encounters helped me find myself as the Sixties blurred into the Seventies. In 1969 (after an eventful year that included a breakdown of the mental hospital variety, being booted out of college, my mother's suicide and a particularly disastrous attempt at communal living) I returned to Binghamton to convalesce. There I met Ken Jacobs, an avant-garde filmmaker and cinema professor who was enthusiastic about an art history paper I'd once written that analyzed Bernard Krigstein's "Master Race" (a then obscure, formally complex 1955 comic book story that alluded to the Nazi death camps). Ken took me under his wing and taught me the value of Art that didn't have speech balloons. When I moved to San Francisco in 1970, Bill Griffith, who was just settling there as well, became my closest colleague and confidant. Our friendship gave me needed stability in the land of lotus-eaters. Virtually all the pieces in *Breakdowns* were first published in projects we co-edited, most notably, *Short Order Comix* and *Arcade, The Comix Revue*.

In 1971, I got to know Justin Green, who was then making the masterpiece that opened up confessional autobiography as subject matter for comix. Strung on a long clothesline in his Mission-district cottage were the pages that would become *Binky Brown Meets the Holy Virgin Mary.* Unlike Crumb, who transmuted his personal obsessions into a universal cartoon language, Justin used the psychosexual and Catholic guilt of his personal life as subject matter to be intimately reported in quirkily drawn, tightly composed pages. It let me finally connect the dots in my own psyche: instead of drawing the most appallingly lurid violence I could dream up, I could now locate the atrocities present in the real world that my parents had survived and brought me into.

The 1972 "Maus" strip that came from this eye-opener was drawn in a somewhat more sober style than my earlier comics, but was radical mainly in its content. "Prisoner on the Hell Planet" came later that year, drawn in Justin's cottage, in fact. (Justin had moved out after helpfully warning me not to face my drawing table north, since rays from the nearby Mission Dolores church could interfere with my work.) "Hell Planet" was more complex in its form and style than anything I'd made before, strengthened by its emotional charge and deepened by my new appetite for the "High" arts on the other side of the High-Low class divide. When "Hell Planet" was published, reduced to standard 7" x 10" underground comix format and printed on newsprint, the detailed scratchboard drawings, inspired by German Expressionist art, looked clotted and congested. I began to want better paper and the larger scale that the oversized *Breakdowns* would eventually allow. (Ironically, most readers were exposed to "Hell Planet" in a terminally cramped incarnation when it was later "entered into the deposition" of the small-size *Maus* book.)

My interests began to diverge from an underground comix scene still dominated by sex, dope and transgressive genre stories. I became consumed with finding out how *narrative* comics had to be to be comics at all, infatuated with the cross-pollination of High and Low. It was actually a very short walk from Chester Gould's *Dick Tracy* to German Expressionism...and only a slightly longer stretch to get immersed in Cézanne, Cubism and the entire convulsion that painting went through when photography threatened all of painting's previous premises.

Painters had then begun to poke at *how* things were represented in painting— paint and canvas became subject matter. Experimental filmmakers around me were looking into film as light passing through celluloid at 24 frames per second. Some of this self-reflexive thinking had been deployed to satirical effect in Harvey Kurtzman's 1950's *MAD* and served as a point of departure for me as a cartoonist looking at the "stuff" of his own medium. I looked at how the illusion of time that is created by juxtaposing images on a page might best be ruptured, at how words and pictures interact and—goofily enough—at Zipatone.

Those self-adhesive sheets of pre-printed dot-screens that simulate a gray tone were still a common part of the cartoonist's tool kit in the pre-digital world, and essential for creating color comix covers. (These color separations involved an esoteric, unlamentably lost craft, difficult to explain to the uninitiated, and far removed from the sensual act of painting. One tediously cut and placed the black dot-screen tints on overlays—

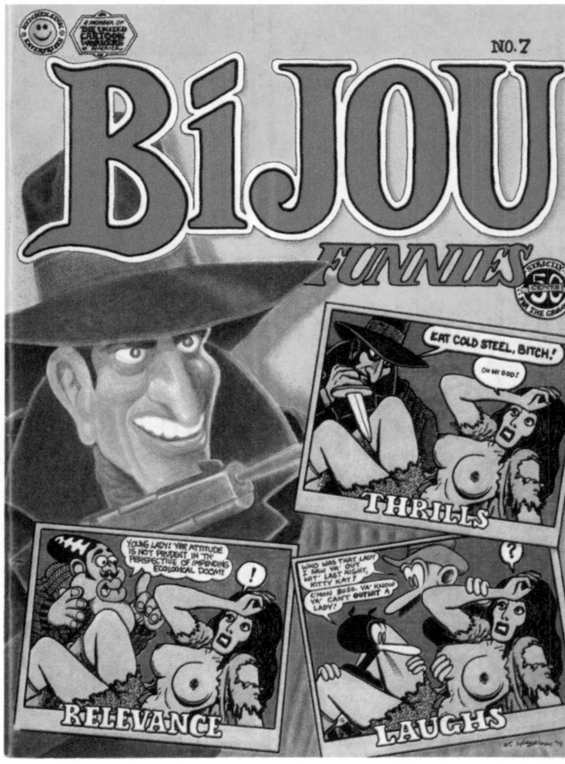
NO.7
BiJOU
FUNNIES
EAT COLD STEEL, BITCH!
OH MY GOD!
THRILLS
YOUNG LADY! YER ATTITUDE IS NOT PRUDENT IN TH' PERSPECTIVE OF IMPENDING ECOLOGICAL DOOM!
!
RELEVANCE
WHO WAS THAT LADY I SAW YA' OUT WIT' LAST NIGHT, KITTY KAT?
C'MON BOSS. YA' KNOW YA' CAN'T OUTWIT A LADY!
?
LAUGHS

ABOVE: **Portrait of the Artist... Photo by Raeanne Rubenstein, 1969**

RIGHT: **Cover, *Bijou Funnies,* #7, 1972 The Viper (with cameos by Skip Williamson and Jay Lynch, my cronies since 1963, when we worked on purple-ink fanzines)**

FACING PAGE.
TOP LEFT: **Flyer for Belier Press, 1977**

BOTTOM RIGHT: **Zipatone overlays for cyan, magenta, yellow and black plates that were used in preparing the covers and endpapers of *Breakdowns***

HOT TORRID SEX!...
WELL, NOW THAT I'VE GOT YOUR ATTENTION...
...I'D LIKE TO SELL YOU MY NEW BOOK!...
BREAKDOWNS
WELL... THERES A DRAWING OF A BLOW JOB ON PAGE TWENTY-TWO!...
AND -UM- NAZIS ARE MENTIONED SEVERAL TIMES!
EEEYUSH!
LISTEN - THIS SLENDER VOLUME CONTAINS THE VERY BEST OF MY LIFE'S WORK!...
...IT'S A COLLECTION OF MY MOST IMPORTANT COMIC-STRIPS FROM VARIOUS UNDERGROUND PUBLICATIONS....
... IN A HIGH-QUALITY FORMAT THAT DISPLAYS MY WORK TO ITS BEST ADVANTAGE:
LARGE (10"×14") SIZE, QUALITY PAPER AND PRINTING, DURABLE BOARD COVERS, 12 COLOR PLATES, AND SEWN BINDING!
EVERYTHING MUST GO!
DRY GOODS SALE
50% OFF
INCIDENTALLY, THIS IS WHAT SOME CRITICS HAVE HAD TO SAY ABOUT SOME PIECES IN THIS BOOK!...
"... astonishing graphic ingenuity, possibly some philosophic profundity. [Spiegelman's strips] bid fair to bring the medium in line with the experimental high art of our age."
David Kunzle, THE NEW REPUBLIC
"Above all, his drawing is full of invention and wit ... doing any number of imaginative things to transcend the convention of the rigidly rectangular panel."
Thomas Albright, SAN FRANCISCO CHRONICLE
"Innovative, boundary-stretching ... he has rethought the possibilities inherent in the comic strip, the narrative form itself..."
Mike Reynolds, THE BERKLEY BARB
"Spiegelman is obsessed with inventing new ways to read and structure comics. A stylistic switch-hitter, without a regular cast of characters, each of Spiegelman's strips is a tightly wrought bundle of ideas."
J. Hoberman, NATIONAL SCREW
"...Never tell the customer 'We've got it, if you want it.'... Use the words NEW or FREE..." -Mail Order Handbook.
WE'VE GOT IT, IF YOU WANT IT!
BREAKDOWNS
NEW?
FREE??
$8.95
From Maus to Now. An anthology of strips by art spiegelman...
BREAKDOWNS An anthology of strips by art spiegelman
DE LUXE EDITION
LARGE 10"×14" FORMAT
BOARD COVERS • SEWN BINDING
TWELVE COLOR PLATES!
AS A LOVER OF COMICS AND FINE BOOKS YOU CAN ORDER YOUR COPY NOW FOR ONLY $8.95!
$8.95 FOR A GODDAMN JOKE-BOOK?!!!
ANYHOW- WE'VE GOT IT IF YOU WANT IT!
BREAKDOWNS!
Belier Press
P.O. Box C, Gracie Sta.
New York, N.Y. 10028
Please RUSH me ______ copy/copies of BREAKDOWNS @ $ 9.95 per copy ($8.95 plus $1.00 postage and handling) I certify that I am an adult, 18 years of age or older and enclose full payment.
Name:
Address:
City: State:
Zip Code:

one overlay for each of the four color printing inks: cyan, magenta, yellow and black. When the tints were placed at the wrong angle, the result was a dreaded, rippled "moiré" pattern.) Anyway, contemplating this process while plucking tiny stray pieces of Zipatone off my clothes led to "Zip-a-tunes and Moiré Melodies," first published as a small 16-page booklet designed to look vaguely like a Thirties "Tijuana Bible" porno comic. This later steered me toward the complex covers and endpapers of *Breakdowns*. Suffice it to say, the fact that comics were printed objects had become part of my subject matter.

"Don't Get Around Much Anymore," drawn over several months in 1973, and physically as well as conceptually at the center of *Breakdowns*, was the result of my wrestling match with Cubism. (Only when it was done did I realize that the graphic style I'd distilled for this page looked something like Art Deco, a style that itself owed a lot to Cubism.) It refracted space into panel-sized facets, froze time, and unmoored words from pictures, all with subject matter as dynamic as a bowl of fruit. Like much of my work, it was dismissed by some readers as depressing. The comment depressed me. My cartoonist peers simply greeted the page with crushing indifference, and encouraged me to pursue things more like *Sleazy Scandals of the Silver Screen,* a comic I was working on at about the same time, or the "Real Dream" pages I did after. I had smashed into the wall that separated cartoonists from Artists. Arteests get to be shamans; us cartoonists are mere "communicators." As Chris Ware succinctly put it years later: "When you don't understand a painting, you assume you're stupid. When you don't understand a comic strip, you assume the cartoonist is stupid."

Stupidly, I continued to peer over the High-Low fence and followed "Don't Get Around Much Anymore" with "Ace Hole, Midget Detective." Though I kept derailing its soft-boiled narrative, at least it seemed to have one. The two-faced femmes fatales that Picasso had painted in the Twenties and Thirties seemed like perfect analogs to the dames Hammett, Chandler and Cain were writing about in the pulps of the same period. The density of ideas compacted into Ace Hole's eight pages resulted from the economic downturn that hit the underground comix "business" in the early Seventies, just when I'd hit my stride. A new head comix publisher, who hadn't yet heard the bad news, committed himself to the second issue of *Short Order Comix,* and I thought it might be my last and best chance to do an extended piece, unfettered, before the whole system tanked. I crammed all the scattered notes and notions about comics that I'd been squirreling away into one eight-page story—one of the longest pieces I ever did before the 300-page *Maus*. I changed the tagline that had been on *Short Order*'s first cover ("Our Motto: No Story Over Four Pages!") to acknowledge the achievement.

In 1970, I'd contributed a dank one-pager about necrophilia to the first issue of *Young Lust*, a popular X-rated parody of Romance genre comics. Four years later, I returned to the magazine, site of that youthful indiscretion, with "Little Signs of Passion." The full-color issue, a rarity at the time, attracted first-rate work by an A-list of underground comix artists. But even in that context, my "deconstruction" (to use a word I didn't know back in 1974) of love stories was not something its Adults Only audience seemed adult enough to embrace.

Many of the artists in that issue of *Young Lust* (Robert Crumb, Kim Deitch, Justin Green, Bill Griffith and Spain Rodriguez) became the core of *Arcade,* a short-lived (1975–1976, R.I.P.) quarterly that tried to function as a lifeboat when the San Francisco comix schooner started to sink. Almost all the pieces I did for *Arcade*—like "Cracking Jokes," the nonfiction comics-format essay on humor that appeared in the first issue

BREAKDOWNS
cyan
magenta
yellow
black
From Maus to Now. An anthology of strips by art spiegelman...

and "The Malpractice Suite," an appropriation (another term I didn't know back then) of inert *Rex Morgan* newspaper strips in the penultimate sixth issue—ended up in *Breakdowns*. In fact, the only thing I did for the magazine that did not make it into the book was "Some Boxes for the Salvation Army," a stillborn project, the remains of which I dumped into *Arcade,* laying it out like a sketchbook of random panels when the deadline loomed. Jealous of my independent filmmaker pals who could shoot footage and edit it after, I wanted to do the same in comics. I reasoned that I could shuffle panels and sequences around after drawing them as long as I used same-size panels on a grid. I could interweave memories, story fragments and ideas in different styles to mimic the non-chronological way the mind works. It sounded like it was worth a try, but unfortunately, I was too scattered a young %@#$!! to draw enough "footage" to quite find out at the time.

In the middle of *Arcade*'s brief run I moved back to New York City and resumed a weekly relationship with Topps Gum. In 1977, Woody Gelman, still the Creative Director of Topps, decided to expand Nostalgia Press, the small publishing house he ran on the side. He asked me if there was any book I ever dreamed of doing, and *Breakdowns* got rolling. But the dream got smashed—like so many American dreams—when Elvis Presley died. Woody, believing he could sell a billion copies of a quickie Elvis memorial poster book, invested in a forest of paper. By the time it became obvious that he'd vastly over-extended himself, *Breakdowns* was already printed. An embarrassed Woody was reluctant to pay the bill and bring the book out. I was devastated, but Jeff Rund, a purveyor of fine bondage and pornography books who had just published a Crumb anthology, generously came to my rescue, explaining to the printer: "I don't understand two thirds of the shit in this book, but anyone who could do that 'Maus' strip and the thing about his mother's suicide deserves a break."

So, with an errata sticker explaining the change of proprietorship, *Breakdowns* got published in 1978. Though to say it was "published" is an exaggeration: five thousand copies had roiled off the press, but almost half of those were unusable. The printers, in a woozy all-nite session, had let black ink glop all over the "Little Signs of Passion" pages, screwing up the mechanical reproduction while ogling the hardcore images of human reproduction. In any case, there was barely any demand for the copies that were bound and offered for distribution. Years later they were still being peddled through small ads in *Raw,* the magazine of avant-garde comics that I co-edited with Françoise Mouly in the Eighties.

The long *Maus* book that followed after *Breakdowns* was originally serialized in the pages of *Raw*. The magazine was shaped by the

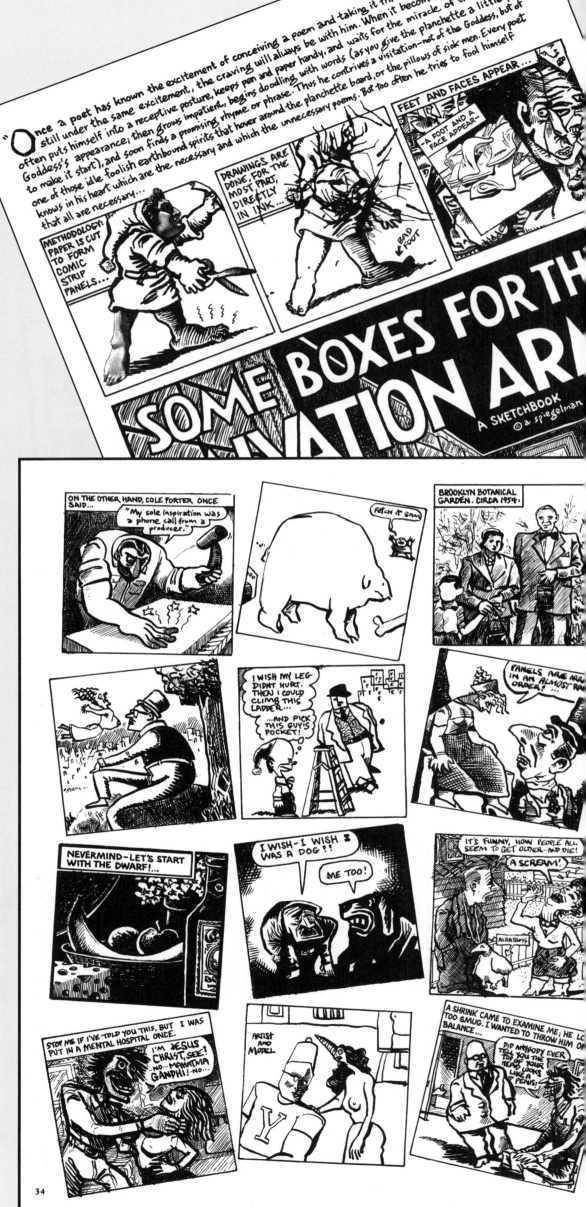

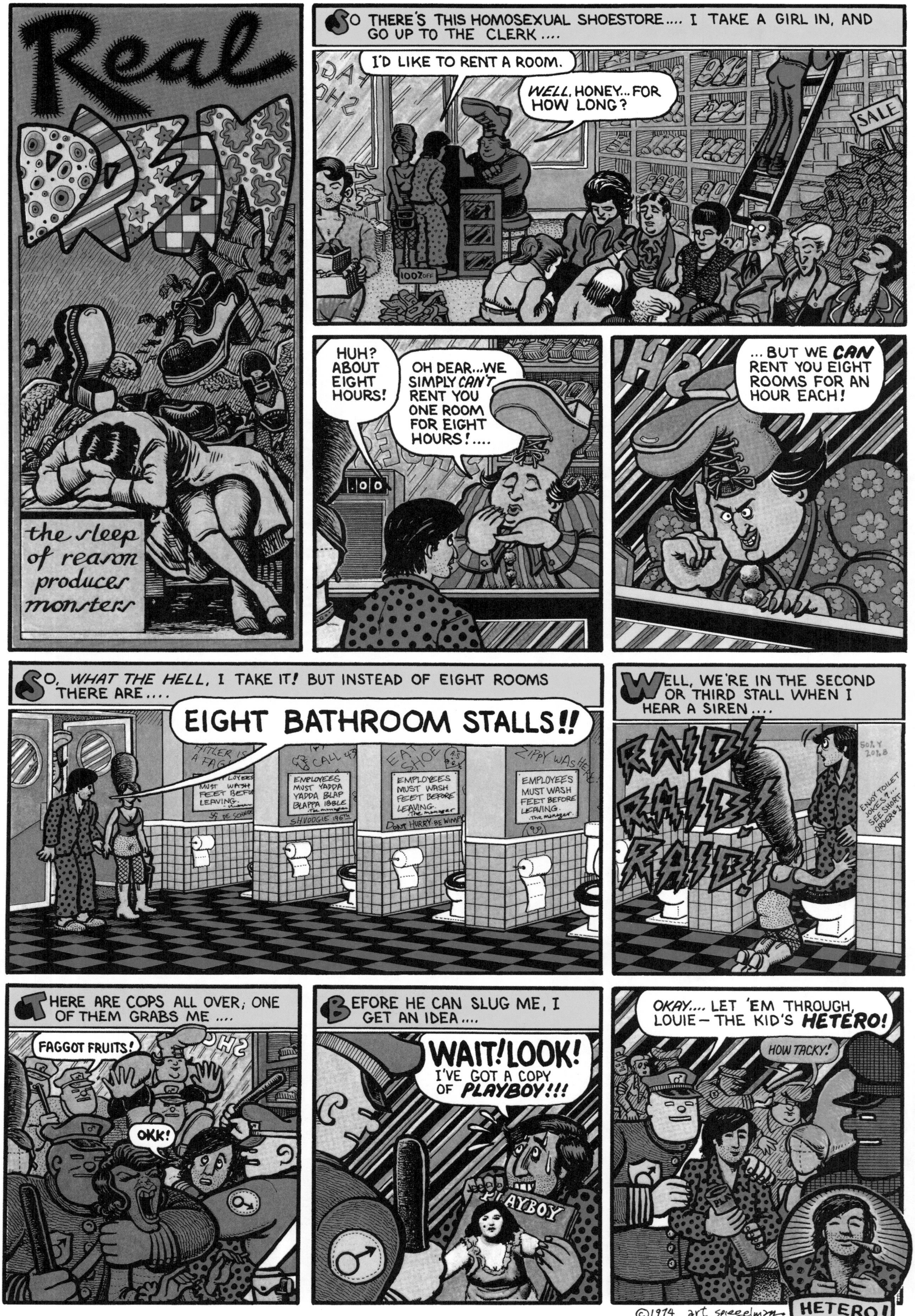
Real
the sleep of reason produces monsters
SO THERE'S THIS HOMOSEXUAL SHOESTORE.... I TAKE A GIRL IN, AND GO UP TO THE CLERK....
I'D LIKE TO RENT A ROOM.
WELL, HONEY... FOR HOW LONG?
SALE
100% OFF
HUH? ABOUT EIGHT HOURS!
OH DEAR...WE SIMPLY CAN'T RENT YOU ONE ROOM FOR EIGHT HOURS!....
...BUT WE CAN RENT YOU EIGHT ROOMS FOR AN HOUR EACH!
SO, WHAT THE HELL, I TAKE IT! BUT INSTEAD OF EIGHT ROOMS THERE ARE....
EIGHT BATHROOM STALLS!!
EMPLOYEES MUST YADDA YADDA BLAP BLAPPA IBBLE
EMPLOYEES MUST WASH FEET BEFORE LEAVING. -The manager
EMPLOYEES MUST WASH FEET BEFORE LEAVING. -The manager
EAT SHOE
ZIPPY WAS HERE
DON'T HURRY. BE WIMPY
WELL, WE'RE IN THE SECOND OR THIRD STALL WHEN I HEAR A SIREN....
RAID! RAID! RAID!
THERE ARE COPS ALL OVER; ONE OF THEM GRABS ME....
FAGGOT FRUITS!
OKK!
BEFORE HE CAN SLUG ME, I GET AN IDEA....
WAIT! LOOK! I'VE GOT A COPY OF PLAYBOY!!!
PLAYBOY
OKAY.... LET 'EM THROUGH, LOUIE — THE KID'S HETERO!
HOW TACKY!
HETERO!

aesthetics and format of *Breakdowns*, combined with Françoise's sense and her sensibility. It was she who dragged me, kicking and screaming, to start *Raw* as a showcase for what comics could be after I'd vowed never to do such a thing again in the wake of *Arcade*! I had first met Françoise when I was putting *Breakdowns* together and she got curious about its production. She mastered the arcane art of hand-cut Zipatone separations after the cursory two-minute explanation I gave her before heading out for a day at Topps. At the end of that day, I returned to find that she had flawlessly completed the separation I was working on. Naturally, dear reader, I married her.

Although *Breakdowns* figures prominently in my life and my development as an artist, I was still startled when Pantheon expressed interest in re-issuing the book. I couldn't help but worry that, once the scarcity factor was removed, Pantheon would be lucky to sell as many copies of this edition as I'd sold of the 1978 book. I didn't want my editors to think they had some red-hot commodity on their hands—like, say, an Elvis Presley poster book—simply because of the success of *Maus*. In fact, it was the resounding lack of response to *Breakdowns* that led directly to the 300-page *Maus*.

Believing that comics were a medium designed for print, I thought that if I kept following the trajectory I was on I'd again be reduced to passing out leaflets on street corners. Instead, I applied the lessons I'd learned while thwarting narrative, spinning them in reverse to make a flowing story, since I dreamed of a comic book that was long enough to need a bookmark.

At any rate, my editor at Pantheon had to listen to my fears that the "hardcore," sexually explicit panels in "Little Signs of Passion"—though not exactly prurient in their context—could still keep the book off-limits for many mainstream booksellers thirty years later. His response, "Huh, you mean the *naughty* bits?" left me feeling like a hick. I know that America has changed dramatically—perhaps even cataclysmically—over the past thirty years, and I know the country's moral center is located somewhere between Janet Jackson's nipple and Paris Hilton's clit…it's just that I can't figure out exactly where.

Still, I'm glad to see *Breakdowns* get a new spin around the block, now that comics are thriving while the rest of America turns to shit. The discoveries I made while working on the strips in that book have somehow been absorbed by those interested in stretching the boundaries of comics over the past thirty years, even if only second or third hand. As a result, some may look at *Breakdowns* as a mere artifact of its time. But for me, it's a manifesto, a diary, a crumpled suicide note and a still-relevant love letter to a medium I adore.

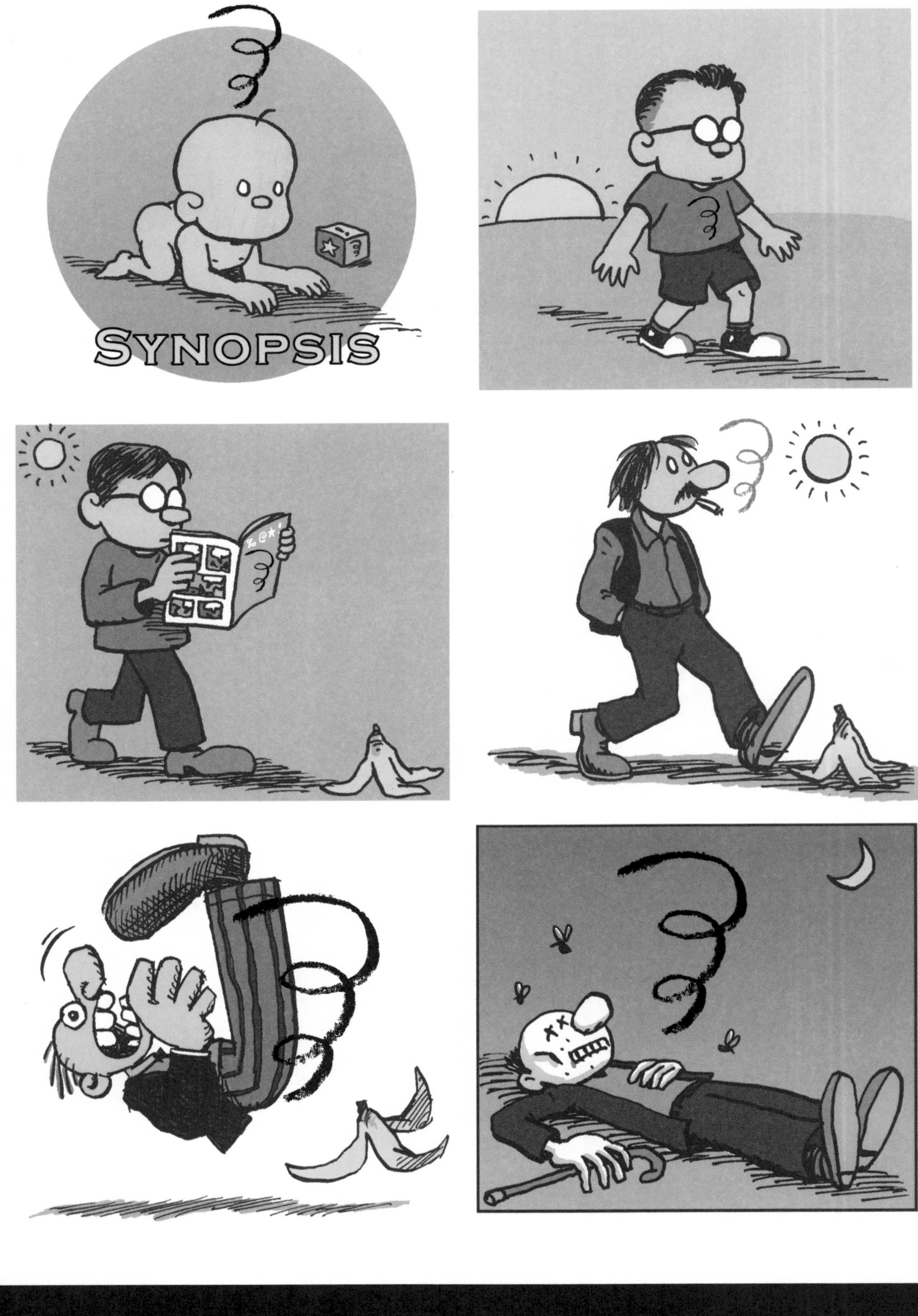
SYNOPSIS

art spiegelman
nyc. 2007

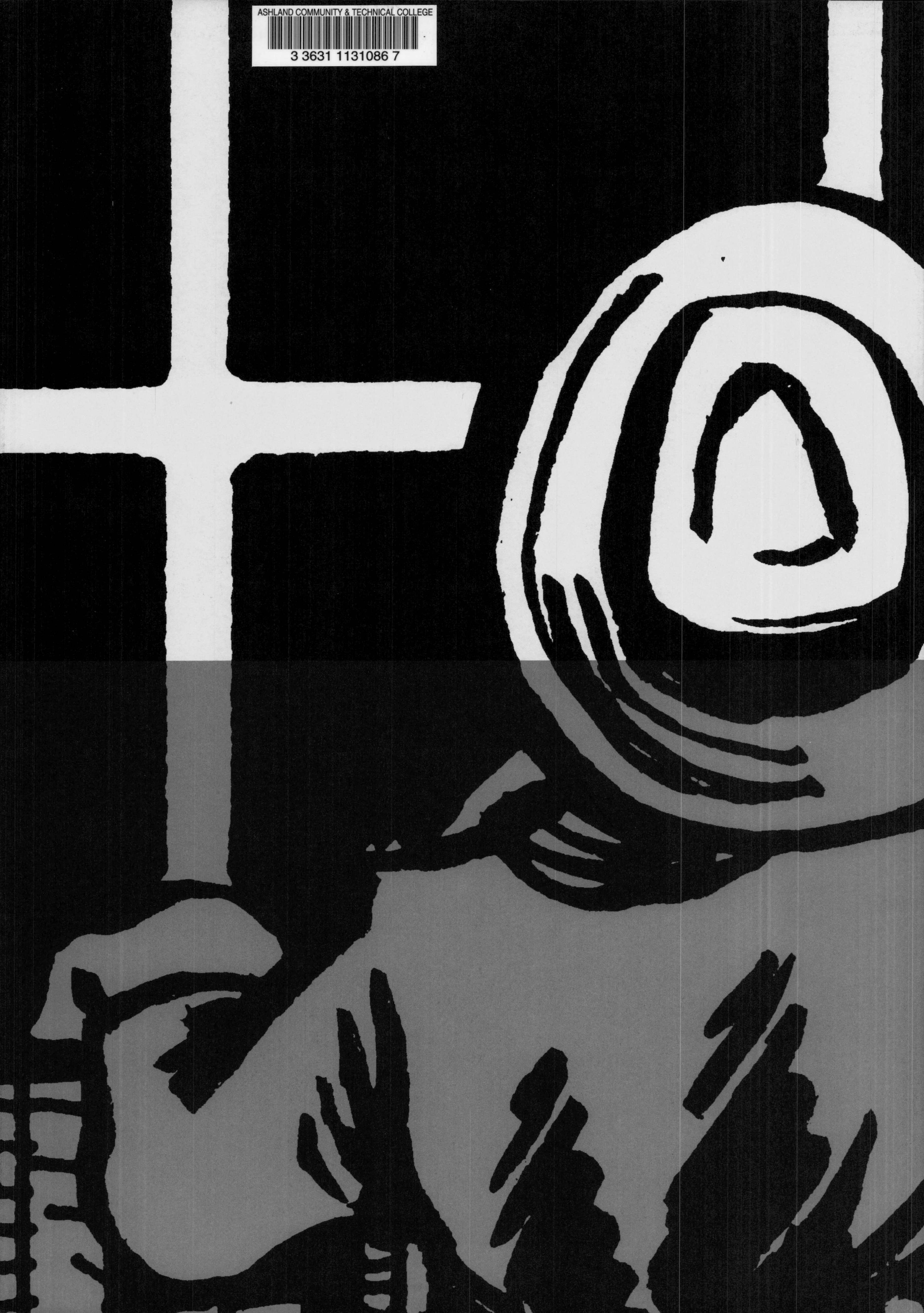